T0094564

FIRE THE BASTARDS!

FIRE
THE
BASTARDS!

by Jack Green

Introduction by Steven Moore

Dalkey Archive Press
Champaign / Dublin / London

The text of *Fire the Bastards!* is in the Public Domain. It first appeared as a three-part article in *newspaper* nos. 12 (24 February 1962), 13 (25 August 1962), and 14 (10 November 1962), pp. 1-76.
Introduction © 1992 by Dalkey Archive Press
Quotations from *The Recognitions* © 1955, 1983 by William Gaddis

Library of Congress Cataloging-in-Publication Data

Green, Jack, 1928-
Fire the bastards! / by Jack Green ; introduction by Steven Moore. -- 2nd ed.
    p. cm.
Includes bibliographical references.
ISBN 978-1-56478-609-8 (pbk. : alk. paper)
    1.   Gaddis, William, 1922-1998. Recognitions. 2.   Gaddis, William, 1922-1998--Criticism and interpretation--History. 3. Book reviewing--United States--History--20th century. I. Title.
PS3557.A28R433 2012
813'.54--dc23
                              2011041190

All rights reserved
First edition, November 1992
Second edition, January 2012

Partially funded by a grant from the Illinois Arts Council, a state agency, and by the University of Illinois at Urbana-Champaign

www.dalkeyarchive.com

Cover: design and composition by Danielle Dutton, photo by Martin Dworkin, courtesy of Bernard Looks
Printed on permanent/durable acid-free paper and bound in the United States of America

Introduction to the 1992 Edition   by Steven Moore

There are two reasons for reprinting Jack Green's *Fire the Bastards!* in book form thirty years after its original appearance as a three-part series in an underground magazine: because it is the first sustained commentary on one of the greatest novels of our time, and because it raises disturbing questions about the book-review media that are as pertinent today as they were thirty years ago. William Gaddis's reputation has improved over those intervening years: *The Recognitions* (1955) was followed by *J R* (1975) and *Carpenter's Gothic* (1985), a body of work that has firmly established Gaddis as one of the most significant American novelists of the postwar period. The review media, on the other hand, hasn't improved; if anything, it has degenerated, and Green's essay is invaluable for under-standing why—a topic I'll take up in the second part of this introduction.

1

The magazine that first published this piece was called simply *newspaper*, a one-man operation written, typed (in lower case and without punctua-tion), mimeographed, and distributed by someone who called himself Jack Green (a pseudonym). Green was born in or around 1928, son of Helen Grace Carlisle, author of *The Merry, Merry Maidens* and other novels. His stepfather was a textbook editor at Harcourt, Brace—coinci-dentally Gaddis's publisher. Green attended high school in Darien, Connecticut; a classmate remembers him as "a mathematical prodigy with a tremendous wit and facility for the piano." He entered Princeton in 1947, where he majored in music, but apparently he left without a degree. In the early fifties he lived in Greenwich Village, studied the psychological theories of Wilhelm Reich, and worked on trying to perfect various gambling systems. In October 1954, as he writes in his autobiographical essay "insurance company days" (*newspaper* 15 [1963?]: 7-15), he "came back from france to newyork hollowcheeked from learning how to lose at roulette" and decided to get a job as an actuary for Metropolitan Life, reasoning "if i must be a gambler, why not work for the house?" In this engaging essay Green recounts his frustrating two and a half years there, ending on a payday in the spring of 1957 when he

> took the cash, down the elevator and out! . . . went to madisonsquare fountain instead   i felt bright, feverish   tore off necktie & dress shirt, flung in fountain   walked home in t-shirt, feeling great   took the razor, the clock, & the mirror & threw them out the window

He then changed his name to Jack Green, perhaps taken from Jack Green's Card—a horse-racing tip sheet of the 1940s. Supporting himself as a free-lance proofreader—by all accounts a quick and accurate one—he started *newspaper*, which he had been planning since his insurance company days. It played a central role in his life from 1957 to 1965, during which time he produced seventeen issues. Appearing at irregular intervals, most issues were filled with his own writing, for even though he welcomed submissions, only a handful of outside material appeared during the entire run: a few poems and prose sketches, one issue (#6) reprinting Jack Jones's essay "To the End of Thought" and the next mostly filled with responses to Jones's piece. But Green's own writings showed great variety: there were many articles on Reich and especially on his persecution by the U.S. Food & Drug Administration, many book reviews (often a few words of straightforward praise followed by sample extracts, letting the books speak for themselves, as it were), scornful examples from the media of the time (especially *Esquire* and the *Village Voice*), articles on dodging the draft, the pointlessness of voting (backed with mathematical equations), on four-handed piano compositions, on peyote (reprinted in Seymour Krim's anthology *The Beats* [1960]), and on anything else that struck his fancy or (more often) infuriated him as yet another example of hypocrisy and mendacity.

In later years—specifically in a pamphlet jokingly called *newspaper* 18 published in 1979—Green apologized for what he considered the "bad writing" of issues #1-17 and retracted his "sales pitch in #8 for peyote and LSD"; but *newspaper* is a bracingly eclectic and fiercely independent example of little-magazine journalism at its best. After Green ceased publication in 1965 with #17, critic Donald Phelps wrote an "Obit of a Sort" (collected in his *Covering Ground: Essays for Now* [New York: Croton, 1969], 208-12) in which he called it "New York's best newspaper" for providing "a running commentary, drily attentive, on current America." Distinguishing "the tough, witty clarity of Green's surveillance" from "the formless, characterless spewing of the less talented 'underground' self-chroniclers," Phelps praises Green's "firmly intelligent critical integrity" and assumes "*newspaper* will continue, metamorphosized—for, one hopes, many good years—in the person of its editor and author." But this apparently was not the case; aside from the *newspaper* #18 of 1979, Green seems to have published only an occasional pamphlet of punning prose: something called *I'm Going Dancing with Lesly Lesby* (1970?), which I've not seen; something else called *Preliminary Edition* (1982), which seems to be a revision-in-progress of *Lesly Lesby* (hard to tell), and most recently, *Snaps* (1991), a mélange of commentary, puns, book reviews, and scenes from Greenwich Village life. (*Preliminary Edition* and *newspaper* #18 were accompanied by separate pamphlets explaining all the references and allusions in these pieces; all of these works—except for *Lesly Lesby*—are available free of charge by writing to Green: P.O. Box 3—Cooper Station, New York, NY 10003.)

The format of *newspaper* was unusual in many ways. It was typewritten and mimeographed by Green himself on heavy, legal-sized beige paper in (according to Phelps) "a soot ink of Green's own composition," and stapled in the top lefthand corner. (Unfortunately, the paper has a high acid content, for surviving copies are brown and brittle with age; another ten years and they will crumble at the touch.) Green didn't use any punctuation (except in quoted matter): no capital letters, few apostrophes, with spaces at the end of sentences instead of periods (unless the line ended flush right), compound words closed up, with spaces between paragraphs rather than indentation. The purpose, Phelps feels, "is not only to disarm the reader, but to liberate Green's voice, by eliminating the most familiar and most innocuous-seeming, therefore the most inhibiting, conventions." Green himself gave this explanation in #2 in response to complaints about the lack of punctuation in #1:

> other publishers use page makeup mostly to conceal the fact that in writing one man is speaking to another, as face makeup & formal clothes are used to conceal it that man is naked before life   also,

> most nonfiction writing is styled so the reader can swill it down
> without chewing it   your teeth gone?   my lack of capitals &
> periods fits my use of incomplete sentences (breaths) and flexible
> stops—what could be less important?   if a thing is unimportant
> you should do it your way not the other persons   also if it is
> important

Copies were sold for a quarter in Greenwich Village bookstores and by subscription; few libraries today have the journal, so apparently it wasn't very successful in this regard or in any financial sense.

Gaddis's *Recognitions* was a recurring topic from the very first issue. Green learned of the novel from a review in the *New Yorker* shortly after publication in 1955, and though he admits that he had some difficulty adjusting to it at first, by 1957 he was convinced it was "a great work of art, the best novel ever written in America" (#1 [4 December 1957]: 5). Noting that the book was being remaindered, he printed four long selections from it to encourage readers to pick it up. There were brief references to the novel in #2 (1958) and #8 (1959), and in 1960 came #10, a 32-page "Quote-Précis of William Gaddis's *The Recognitions*." In #11 (3 June 1961), Green announced

> the quoteprecis (#10) was the 1st of at least 5 long issues on
> gaddis   the articles on references & crossreferences in *the recog-*
> *nitions*   & attacking the reviews that prevented the book from
> being accepted as the masterpiece it is   are far from finished &
> there will again be a long delay between issues

"Fire the Bastards!" occupied three issues (#12-14) published over a nine-month period in 1962 and was continuously paginated: 76 pages of scorching invective and exhaustive analyses of every review *The Recognitions* received. But he didn't stop there: he also took out a full-page ad in the *Village Voice* (reproduced on the following page) to publicize the newly released Meridian paperback edition of *The Recognitions* as well as *newspaper* #12. There was speculation then (and for many years after) that Gaddis not only paid for the ad himself, but that he was none other than Jack Green writing under a pseudonym. (Later there was even speculation that Gaddis, after "failing" with *The Recognitions,* began writing under the pseudonym of Thomas Pynchon.) Gaddis was naturally pleased at Green's prodigious efforts ("Here at last—a la revanche!" he wrote to his editor Aaron Asher upon publication of #12) but undoubtedly kept his distance from the project (as he has with subsequent criticism of his work). He had met Green in 1959 and would run into him occasionally over the years, but he apparently had little to do with "Fire the Bastards!" aside from perhaps loaning Green the original reviews. (Green also supplied Gaddis with a list of typos in the first edition of *The Recognitions* which were corrected in the 1962 Meridian edition and again in 1985 in the Penguin reprint of the novel.)

Despite its limited distribution, "Fire the Bastards!" caused a bit of a stir in the industry, as he records at the end of the essay: "#12 touched a raw nerve, got some action   the establishment surrendered without a fight, admitting its sins with humorous tolerance for itself & those who had no right to be right." However, he goes on to admit "most of the 1962 plugs had only a momentary effect because they were by phonies, insincere jobholders who often hadnt even read the book." Sales of *The Recognitions* were strong enough to justify a second printing of the Meridian paperback in 1963, and in 1964 even the original publisher decided to reprint their hardcover edition (raising the price to $8.50 but ignoring the

THE RECOGNITIONS
by William Gaddis

After 7 years this great novel is finally out in paperback
(Meridian, $2.75 at all bookstores).

"The Recognitions" is a 956-page novel whose main theme is
vanity or forgery—of Old Masters, $20 bills, slings,
personality, everything. It is like a painting with a few
primary figures presented in depth and an army of caricatures
in the background. The main characters are unforgettable and,
as is usually true, give the book most of its greatness. The
minor characters, including the author himself who has a bit
part, are very funny.

Like "Ulysses," Gaddis's book can be read the first time with
enjoyment (my advice: don't work at it) and then reread for
years with increasing fascination. It has an intricate network
of thousands of cross-references which give it a unique
time-sense: as the connections are gradually recognized on
rereading, the book appears to grow like a living being.

The writing itself is excellent. Gutless readers who prefer
judging characters to being judged by them are advised to
stay away from Wyatt and Esme.

"The Recognitions" sold like cold cakes in hardcover because
of stupid reviews by the incompetent, amateurish critics.
Everyone "knows" the critics are no good, but everyone believes
them anyway. For an antidote I offer my article "fire the
bastards!" (Part I is issue no. 12 of "newspaper.") It's a
detailed analysis of the antics of the "Recognitions" reviewers,
on sale at Village bookstores. Or mail me a quarter for it.
A dollar for issues no. 12-15. $5.00 for issues no. 1-20.

Jack Green
Box 114
New York 12

sixty or so corrections Gaddis made for the Meridian edition). But by then the momentum had slowed and *The Recognitions* had once again gone "underground" to remain a "cult" book for another decade.

In 1964, Green wrote an epilogue of sorts (in *newspaper* #16) entitled "gaddis gossipcolumns" in which he concludes the story and regrets his efforts on behalf of Gaddis and Jack Jones's essay. Making special reference to a piece by Jerome Beatty, Jr., in the "Trade Winds" column of *Saturday Review* (21 April 1962, 8-9), Green writes:

> beatty, hogan, macgregor & in *publishers' weekly* (see issue #14) no interest in *the recognitions,* only in the "Gaddis underground" as a 3ring circus   beattys 14th & last paragraph gets around to " 'The Recognitions,' by the way"—that sums it up   hogan:
>
> > According to a hard core of partisans, "The Recognitions" is one of the most important works since Joyce's "Ulysses." I learned long ago never to argue with a hard core of partisans of anything. In this case I shall take their word for it, *and* leave the decision to future literary historians.
>
> (my italics)   decision if gaddis is "as good as Jack Green says he is, or is this just another nine-dollar bill?"   i invited this vulgar flippancy, at gaddis expense & mine, by letting gossipcolumnists interview me
>
> "hard core of partisans"—cf other critics "literary brotherhood," "William Gaddis bandwagon," "William Gaddis Fanclub" with their "enthusiastic admonitions to Read It," "small group of vocal admirers," "subterranean bible," "cult following"   david boroff, suggesting novels "which are not much read these days but deserve to be" (*ny times book review* 6/9/63 3) declines to discuss *the recognitions* because "The cults need little help from me"—there are already "loyal coteries beating the drums"   a 2d line of defense after the fake surrender of 1962   on this line, since those who speak up for gaddis work (or atonal music or *ulysses* or wilhelm reich) are noisy, cultist, ridiculous, it follows that the cultists *and the work* should be quarantined   this was a lie 50 yrs ago & it still is
>
> next step is to defame gaddis personally using the Fanclub as a steppingstone   beatty used what i blabbed to him, that when i quit the insurance company i threw my necktie into the madison-square fountain   gaddis was more reticent   middleman beattys revenge:
>
> > right now [William Gaddis] works in New York for a respectable corporation and he would rather not be identified any further than that. After all, he's got a *job,* and he's probably not about to toss his necktie into the Seagram Building pool.
>
> it was wrong & presumptuous of me to seek publicity for jones & gaddis in ways i wouldnt for myself   i risked interfering with natural growth of acceptance of their work by my "shot in the arm" methods

In the same issue of *newspaper* Green recounts the efforts made to reprint "Fire the Bastards!" in more permanent form. Poet and critic Karl Shapiro asked to reprint it in a special issue of *Prairie Schooner* that was to be devoted to Gaddis's novel. Green agreed reluctantly (because there

x

was no reprint fee: the sponsoring university's yearly income was $20,000,000.00, he noted); as he tells it:

> few months later shapiro was finking about length: "what would you do in a case like this?"   so i prepared a ½length version but came to my senses at the last moment, didnt send it   few months more, shapiro out as editor   (university censors banned a story hed accepted—it was already set in type)   no reprint, no notice there wouldnt be one

Then (from the same issue):

> sent "fire the bastards!" to grove & putnam's . . . grove got the 50000word ms tuesday, sent it back wednesday   putnam's was less hasty—they never answered

Green continued his own work on the references and cross-references in *The Recognitions* (until 1980 when, feeling it would never be "satisfactory," as he put it, he threw it out) but apparently made no further effort to reprint "Fire the Bastards!"

Two offers were made in the early 1980s to reprint the essay, but by then Green was no longer interested. I wanted to reprint it in an anthology of Gaddis criticism that John Kuehl and I were compiling. At that time (mid-1981) we had no idea of Green's whereabouts or whether he was even still alive. Since our prospective publisher expected to see the manuscript in early 1982, I decided we would lose valuable time if we waited until we located Green (assuming he could be located), so I sent a query for information regarding Green to the *New York Times Book Review* (which wasn't published until the following year) and began preparing a new typescript of Green's essay. Feeling that the lack of punctuation was an unnecessary hindrance—and not having read his justification of his practices in *newspaper* #2—I restored capitalization and periods, indented paragraphs, and incorporated a few of his shorter footnotes into the body of the text in parentheses. The content remained exactly the same, only the appearance had changed. Kuehl and I were also concerned about getting this piece (along with the rest of the book) past an editorial board who might be put off by Green's unscholarly tone; we didn't have a contract yet and the eccentric format of Green's essay might have jeopardized our chances of publication.

It wasn't until after I had prepared the typescript that William Gaddis was able to dig up an old address for me; I wrote to Green to ask permission to reprint "Fire the Bastards!" and he wrote back refusing permission, saying that the essay was poorly written. A brief digression is needed at this point to explain the disingenuousness of his refusal. What he didn't mention was the fact that "Fire the Bastards!," like the rest of *newspaper*, was never copyrighted and thus was in the public domain. Legally, we didn't need his permission, for by refusing to copyright his work Green had relinquished all rights to it, had donated it to the public domain. Nor was this an oversight: he was fully aware back in his *newspaper* days that his work was not under copyright, nor was this the first time he had concealed this. The most embarrassing piece in *newspaper* is an epistolary exchange published in #16 between Green and Orion Press. They had signed a contract whereby $20.00 was to be paid to Green "in consideration for permission to reprint" his essay "Peyote" in a forthcoming book called *The Drug Experience,* edited by David Ebin, with the fee payable upon publication. Green chose to interpret the $20.00 fee to be for "permission" to reprint, whether they used the essay or not; the editors decided not to use "Peyote" after all, but when the book was published in 1961 Green wrote demanding his fee. They wrote back explaining that the fee was understood to be for *use* of the essay, not merely for *permission* to use, but Green threatened to sue and eventually Orion, just to get rid of him, paid the $20.00. (This wrangling occupied a year and a half's time.) At the end of the last letter, there is a snide postscript in parentheses by Green: "(ps 'peyote' is not copyrighted)." In other words, he knew that the whole legal exchange was a farce because permission for "peyote" was not his to give or withhold.

His pharisaical insistence on the letter of the law at the expense of its spirit in this exchange is disheartening; when he adds that, in effect, he was simply bluffing, he becomes guilty of the same sort of mendacity he accuses in others. It must be said, however, that this particular incident is a deviation; throughout the rest of *newspaper,* Green seems to have strictly maintained the uncompromising high standards he set for himself and expected in others.

Back to our story. I was deeply disappointed in Green's refusal, partly because I had spent three months preparing the typescript (with much research verifying and adding to his bibliography), and partly because I felt Green's essay was the cornerstone of Gaddis criticism and deserved to be better known. (I've lost track of how many times I've photocopied my set of *newspaper* #12-14 for other Gaddis critics.) So I wrote back remonstrating with him, offering to let him add a headnote explaining his current opinion of the work, and told him that I didn't think it was poorly written at all, especially in the more conventional typescript I had prepared. That did it. The fact that I had "revised" his work (as he put it) without his permission enraged Green. He wrote back to accuse me of "barefaced impudence," again refused permission, and forbade me to write him again "on this or any other subject." That last injunction kept Green in self-imposed ignorance of the actual circumstances of this project. Had I known beforehand of Green's whereabouts, I certainly would have asked his permission to put his essay in more conventional form. Had he allowed me to write again, I would have explained this and cheerfully offered to throw my three-months' labor out the window and submit his original with the rest of our manuscript and take my chances with the editorial board. But it seemed pointless to remonstrate further, or to ask Gaddis to intervene. As anyone who's dealt with a difficult person knows, these are no-win situations: goodwill gestures are twisted into malicious ones, the hand that feeds is viciously bitten, generous motives are assumed to mask selfish, ulterior motives, and so on. Even though we suspected Green had no legal right to his work, we decided to honor his undoubted ethical right to his own work. When the book was accepted and published by Syracuse University Press in 1984 as *In Recognition of William Gaddis,* I insisted on dedicating it to Green (Kuehl wanted to dedicate it to James Laughlin of New Directions), but even this "jolly (& deserved, really)" dedication, as Gaddis wrote me, was misinterpreted by Green as a deliberate insult on my part and he asked Kuehl to remove the dedication in any future printings.

In early 1982, John O'Brien also asked to reprint "Fire the Bastards!" in a special issue of his *Review of Contemporary Fiction* to be devoted to Gaddis's work, and he too was refused permission, Green again explaining that it was poorly written but that he hoped to issue revised versions of some of his early work someday.

Ten years later, deeply troubled by the current book-reviewing situation, O'Brien and I decided "Fire the Bastards!" was too important to remain unknown, and that Green's personal feelings regarding his work were heavily outweighed by cultural considerations regarding his essay's value for the ongoing debate over the inadequacy of the review media vis-à-vis innovative fiction. Green was not consulted during the preparation of this new edition, but bearing in mind his earlier objections, this version follows his original in form as well as content, with only a few modifications: footnotes are set in smaller type, section titles are set in boldface, underlined words and titles set in italics, and some extraneous matter (such as an announcement on the first page for the then-forthcoming Meridian edition of *The Recognitions*) deleted. In all other respects, this edition follows the original slavishly: even this sans-serif typeface resembles that of Green's typewriter, and this elongated format recalls *newspaper's* 8½ x 14 sheets. Since the original essay was continuously paginated and apparently broken into three parts more for the convenience of publication than for any organic reason, the divisions between parts are not indicated here. (For the record, part 2 began with the attack on Granville Hicks's *New York Times* review near the top of p. 26, and part 3 began with the section entitled "the erudition cliche" in the middle of p. 52.) Although the material is in the public domain, a standard royalty is being reserved for Green should he ever wish to claim it.

2

As bad as the review "racket" may have seemed to Green in 1962, it is far worse today for innovative fiction. Green notes that *The Recognitions* received fifty-five reviews—an astounding number for a huge, difficult novel by an unknown writer. (Some of these reviews were syndicated to several newspapers, raising the number even higher.) A similar novel published today would be lucky to get a fourth of that number. Finding a contemporary parallel to *The Recognitions* is difficult, but for purposes of comparison, consider the reception of William T. Vollmann's 1987 novel *You Bright and Risen Angels* (Atheneum). Like *The Recognitions,* it was a long, complex first novel from a young, unknown writer and was as far removed from the prevailing fiction trends of the mid-1980s as *The Recognitions* was from those of the mid-1950s. By any measure it was a brilliant debut, and even in a year that included several excellent American novels— John Barth's *Tidewater Tales,* Stanley Elkin's *Rabbi of Lud,* Joseph McElroy's *Women and Men,* Alexander Theroux's *An Adultery*—Vollmann's was arguably the most daring and creative novel of the year. How many reviews did this superb contribution to American literature receive in this country? Just ten. Three pre-publication trade journals reviewed it— *Publishers Weekly* (positive), *Kirkus Reviews,* and *Library Journal* (both negative, though a "fascinating flop," the latter concedes)—and there were brief mentions in *USA Today* and something called *Spectrum* (both noncommittal, but mildly positive). It received only five full-length reviews: in the *New York Times Book Review, San Francisco Chronicle* (Vollmann was living in that city at the time), *San José Mercury News, Providence Sunday Journal,* and the *Anniston* (Alabama) *Star.* Except for Jeff Riggenbach's positive notice in the *San José Mercury News,* the reviews were mixed, each finding as many faults as virtues in Vollmann's work. But Riggenbach's review appeared in the science fiction column, which means it would have been ignored by most literary readers. (*You Bright and Risen Angels* is science fiction only in the broad sense that Burroughs's *Naked Lunch* or Pynchon's *Gravity's Rainbow* is.) The final result of this scanty attention is that a general reader interested in innovative fiction wouldn't have seen a *single* review that responded to *You Bright and Risen Angels* as it deserved and/or that recommended it strongly. Such readers learn of such books only by accident, by word of mouth, learning about it (as most kids learn of sex) from the streets, as it were.

Vollmann's novel received far fewer reviews than Gaddis's partly because the review media is less receptive to such work than it was thirty-five years ago, and partly because circumstances have changed for the worse. Many newspaper and book review supplements have reduced the amount of space available for reviews; some (like the *Saturday Review* and the *New York Herald Tribune*) no longer exist, others (like *Harper's*) no longer review books; many book review editors are journalists with non-literary backgrounds and conventional tastes; and there is a field-wide tendency to ignore literary fiction in favor of mainstream books. New product by the likes of Stephen King or Danielle Steel is now reviewed where in the past they would have been passed over in silence, if not with contempt; nowadays it is the literary fiction (and especially translations) that is passed over in silence.

Nor do reviewers seem to be any better qualified than they were in Green's day. But such complaints are hardy perennials, returning every publishing season in the mouths of disgruntled authors and publishers. (Readers too would complain if they were better acquainted with the book-reviewing process.) The problem is exacerbated today due to the sheer number of worthwhile books crying out for review. The proliferation of independent presses over the last ten years, taking up the literary slack of New York publishers and in many cases surpassing them in literary titles, has led to an unprecedented amount of quality literature being made available. But the interested reader learns of only a fraction of this work, and usually only those token literary books still published in New York by the big conglomerates. Where does a reader turn to keep abreast of literary fiction? The *New York Times Book Review,* once the obvious choice (though Green calls it "the worst bookreview section in the world" [31]), now treats books as a branch of the entertainment industry and is the last place anyone would look for wide coverage of innovative fiction; besides, like the *New York Review of Books,* its emphasis is on nonfiction. The *Washington Post Book World* makes a greater effort to cover quality fiction, but hasn't room for extensive coverage. The *American Book Review* and the *Review of Contemporary Fiction* probably review more such fiction than anyone else, but *ABR* is always seasons behind publication dates (by which time many bookstores have already returned the books to their distributors) and *RCF,* published only three times a year, lacks the immediacy of a weekly or monthly journal. Green said the worst review is no review at all, and too many quality books get no reviews at all in the places that matter most. If they don't get reviewed, they won't be stocked in bookstores, and thus the reader never learns about them, unless he or she comes across them by chance on a remainders table a year or two later.

The fact that Gaddis's *Recognitions* did eventually rise to the surface after being torpedoed by the critics may seem to argue that book reviews aren't all that important: worthy books will prevail, forgotten masterpieces will be rediscovered and take their places in the canon. But a complacent confidence that future literary historians will sort things out is damaging to both writers and our culture. Instead of joining the ranks of our leading novelists, William Gaddis spent the next twenty years of his career doing public relations work, scripting films for the army, writing speeches for corporate executives, and other deadening jobs. It is something of a miracle that he was able to write *J R* during those same twenty years, though *J R* includes failed, suicidal writers who are more representative of neglected artists. Even when "forgotten masterpieces" are rediscovered and reprinted, they are treated not as active artworks but as historic relics. Innovative art always challenges the status quo and conventional modes of thinking and are meant to be a part of today's cultural dialogue, not fodder for tomorrow's dissertations. As Jack Green points out, "the *real* job of reviewing [is] to see that great books are bought *now*   & not, like *the recognitions* will be, years & years after publication." It is the review media's responsibility to make these works known, but too often it acts as an obstacle course by placing inadequate reviews between the book and its potential readers, or, more and more frequently these days, it acts as a de facto censor by not even bothering to review such books.

It is highly ironic that we live in an Age of Information where, if anything, we risk information-overload on most topics, and yet where there isn't a single, comprehensive source for intelligent, timely coverage of quality fiction. The ills of the book-review media that Green diagnosed are apparently organic and irreversible; it is now impossible to imagine the current media expanding its coverage of this literature. To "fire the bastards!" may once have seemed like a solution, but a more practical one remains to be found.

FIRE THE BASTARDS!

william gaddis's *the recognitions* was published in 1955   its a great novel, as much *the* novel of our generation as *ulysses* was of its   it only sold a few thousand copies because the critics did a lousy job—

—2 critics boasted they didnt finish the book

—one critic made 7 boners   others got wrong the number of pages, year, price, publisher, author, & title

—& other incredible boners like mistaking a diabetic for a narcotics addict

—one critic stole part of his review from the blurb, part from another review

—one critic called the book "disgusting" "evil" "foul-mouthed," needs "to have its mouth washed out with lye soap"   others were contemptuous or condescending

—2 of 55 reviews were adequate   the others were amateurish & incompetent

  failing to recognize the greatness of the book

  failing to convey to the reader what the book is like, what its essential qualities are

  counterfeiting this with stereotyped preconceptions—the standard cliches about a book that is "ambitious," "erudite," "long," "negative," etc

  counterfeiting competence with inhuman jargon

—constructive suggestion: fire the bastards!

i 1st heard of *the recognitions* from a review in the *new yorker*   the reviewer said the book was like *ulysses* but not as good   in his own anonymous condescending & selfdamning words:

  In form, content, length, and richness of imagery, as well as in syntax, punctuation, and even typography, this novel challenges the reader to compare it with Joyce's "Ulysses." So challenged, the reader is obliged to say that while Mr. Gaddis has been very brave, Shem the Penman has won the day.

(posing as "the reader" instead of "i" is a trick to pretend modesty while assuming an undeserved impersonal authority   he means his opinion as a mere human being   or mine or yours or anyones   is sneerable at   but after "the reader" is hired by Authority, paid a few

measly bucks for a few spotty hours reading, "the reader" becomes
    god?   objective?   full of rich status?   or still the same idiot,
playing it safe)

i was lucky not to read a dead indifferent review but a vicious one that
caught my interest   mulish i figured a book could fall short of
ulysses & still be pretty good   so i got it

like the imbecile critics i was rattled at 1st by the length of the book,
over 400000 words   so i started skipping around & reading back-
wards & forwards from the middle   after a few days i was quite
confused   "whats this guy trying to do" id ask my friends   "is he
nuts or has he really got something?"   *a balanced, judicious view*

i was still getting into the book & getting used to the toneddown
narrative style, new to me   but suppose i was a hack reviewer,
educated by years of fakework to think no books worth reading
carefully unless everyones already read it   condemned to review
heaps of mediocre books in less than no time   wouldnt i have had
to   wouldnt i have seized the opportunity to write at the moment of
maximum confusion   wouldnt my inner magician force me to rush
the job without waiting to come to terms with what was new to me
    disguise my ignorance with yawny jargon & clever remarks about
whatever i didnt understand   & for safety, the latest catchphrases
from the Frightened Philistines of the *times* & *saturday review*   &
what if i more or less secretly hated good books?

not being a hack reviewer i could go on reading *the recognitions*
instead of forgetting it amid the 10 most worthless books of the
month   years after, i was still drawn by its fascination & kept rereading it   & i swear by all the work ive done & will do that *the
recognitions* is a great work of art   before the mass public i know of
no great novel that was permanently defeated by the enemies of art.
but it is now possible, in this indifferent decadent time, *and it must not
happen*   for years after the fake reviewers forced gaddis's book into
the remainder piles it was as forgotten as if we had no glorious
publishing industry with glorious receptions rooms & big money for
everyone except writers

with fear & favor

the worst review is no review   blackest marks go to *harper's, new
leader, new republic, a.l.a. booklist,* a few newspapers   & most of the
quarterlies (they were busy measuring henry james fingernails)

but there were reviews in most of the usual outlets   not because
the recognitions is a good book   because harcourt, brace made it
appear   at 1st   a major enterprise of a major publisher   harcourt hoped for an easy success but gave up quick when reviews &
sales looked sour   took very little advertising*

---

*their only *ny times* ad dishonestly quoted a review out of context   *time*
magazine: "U.S. novel writing has a strikingly fresh talent to watch, if not to
cheer."   as quoted: "U.S. novel writing has a strikingly fresh talent to watch"
    this sells books?

the 55 reviews mostly play it safe   moderation   by moderation, i
seem to mean mediocrity   lack of genuine response   excluding,
as sound statistical method dictates, the critics who didnt happen to
read the book before they reviewed it   there were 4 really favorable
reviews & 1 or 2 strongly unfavorable   all the rest are in a narrow
range of more or less "balanced" opinion—ie, they outrageously underrate the book

there were more slightly favorable reviews than slightly unfavorable
ones   now to get technical & show this was *un*favorable   a study
by merritt says ½ the major reviews of an average book are noncommittal & the rest split about 12 to 1 favorable*   he counts faintly
favorable reviews as "favorable" etc   *the recognitions*   using his
criteria   got at best 2 to 1 favorable**   the average book doesnt
sell well   therefore a book that gets less than 12 to 1 favorable will
sell very badly

all-unfavorable reviews may seem more effective & maybe could have
cut the sales of the book from a few thousand to a few hundred.
but why take chances it might backfire   the unconscious of the
20thcentury hater has learned that wild slanders arent necessary.
mild underapproval is enough   & no backfire—who fights the face-
less blobs?

noncommittal review means buying a novels a gamble   whod gamble
$7.50 (the hardcover price) on a book that has some good points, &
some bad points, & some good points, & so on till you fall asleep over
the critics dull prose

that "12 to 1 favorable" is abdication   being noncommittal, the
"balancing" trick, is abdication   "balanced" reviews of a great novel
are indifference (concealed hate) plus tricks   worthless

another abdication when critic abandons pretended interest in whether
a books good   sticks to question, how well will it sell

---

*very courteous to the advertisers   but has been widely criticized, & i join in,
as indicating a bland affability, a refusal to love or hate that has no relation to
the passion for books   a poor substitute for even the wild moralistic reviews of
the 19th century (leRoy c merritt "the pattern of modern book reviewing" in
reviews in library book selection wayne univ studies #3 detroit 1958   reviews
& ratings taken from *book review digest*)

**book review digest* listed 4 favorable, 7 noncommittal, 2 unfavorable reviews of
the recognitions   even using the narrow definition of "noncommittal" id say 2
7 & 4, that is, 2 to 1 *un*favorable   the *new yorker* review eg being obviously
unfavorable, not noncommittal   i rated the other 42 reviews   mostly in
smallcity newspapers not listed in *brd*   2 to 1 favorable   so maybe the
smallcity reviewers, dumb as they are, did better   could be, smallcity papers
surrender more naively to advertiser-publishers, are more favorable in general.
could be, smallcity reviewer not scared to death to stick his neck out *too early*
for a controversial book, as of course the cowards on the *times* & *saturday
review* are—it would demonstrate their unreliability, bordering on crankery, to the
fakers who control the bigtime review racket & its side benefits

also, the *ny times* review of *the recognitions* is noncommittal by *brd* standards
but is actually a clever, evil effort to kill a great book "impartially"   the
saturday reviewer was as unfavorable as he was stupid, which is saying a great
deal   & these 2 probably have more influence than the other 53 combined

4

as a highbrow, the critic doesnt ask crudely how much mazuma a book will rake in but whether it will "stir up a storm" & such euphemisms:

> may well become one of the most controversial novels of this or many another year (from edward a bloom's review in the *providence journal*)

> certain to achieve some special sort of notoriety. (morse, *hartford courant*)

> Gaddis' New Book Should Cause Furor (harrison smith)

> First Novel Sure to Stir Up Storm (emerson price)

> Whatever one's opinion of his work, its great power and genuine originality are likely to have considerable influence in the future. (price)

the critics just quoted are good guardians of the peace   to keep "furor" from developing into mass panic, they refrain from making any firm judgments themselves   (price *balances* his "power and original-ity" by implying gaddis is guilty of a bit of counterfeiting, has no compassion, feels utter contempt for mankind)

heres a complete review   this ones contemptuous   all about sales potential & not a word about whether the book is good   its "b w":

> The latest entry in the Thomas Wolfe sweepstakes is a big (956 pages) fellow from the respected Harcourt, Brace stable. The paddock crowd is split on this contender's chances, with the odds running long, about 7-3.
> This is the jockey's first time out on a major track. The rail-birds are speculating that he's still carrying too much weight, but they said that about James Joyce years ago and they said it about Saul Bellow, up on "Augie March," in last year's running of the Wolfe race. "Augie" performed well, too.
> Chances are that if Gaddis doesn't bring in this entry he'll do better in subsequent showings. A talk with the boys in the tack room ought to convince him that he can do better in shorter stretches.
> At $7.50 "The Recognitions" isn't likely to attract much interest from the line at the $2 window.
> The tack room verdict: Keep the jockey and retire the horse.

yes, criminal negligence can be sportive!

to read or not to read

the reason the *nashville tennesseean* must FIRE "b w" or at least return him to the dept he was borrowed from   is that he never read the book he reviewed   the review could have been, & was, written without even opening the book

only 5 or 6 of 55 reviewers of *the recognitions* didn't read it   the other 90% either got through it or theyre too smart for me

FIRE edward wagenknecht of the *chicago tribune* for his confession, or rather boast:

> There are 956 pages in this book, and I must confess that I did not stay until the last had been turned.
>
> What is "The Recognitions" about? Really, I have no idea.
>
> It is not pleasant to be defeated by a book.

but isnt it pleasant to be paid for work you havent done?

> I'm like the Vermont farmer listening to the New Deal spellbinder. "What's he talking about?" his neighbor queried perturbedly. And, quite without perturbation, he replied, "He don't say."
> Gaddis don't say neither. (wagenknecht)

time out while the *chi trib* elects thos e dewey again   how folksy theyre getting in the windy city!   do novelists have to spell out what theyre "talking about"?

FIRE the anonymous hack of the *toronto globe & mail* he didn't finish the book either   headline: It Beats Us

> Frequently we sample a new book, reading a few paragraphs here and there to get the hang of it; but several such samplings left us blanker and blanker. It is a most humiliating thing for a reviewer of upwards of 40 years' experience not to be able to understand a novel, not get even a clue. So the samplings became fewer and farther apart and had stopped when we discovered the able Chicago Tribune man, Edward Wagenknecht, was in the same fix.

"able"!   the provincial disciple acknowledges his master—at gold-bricking   after 40 years experience faking cant he even write his own review?   almost ½ of it is right out of wagenknecht

> Mr. Wagenknecht worked harder at the book than we did because he discovered there is a new cast of characters in every chapter (*toronto globe & mail*)

"—tho there are some carry-overs" (wagenknecht)   does quoting a boner make it true?   in sum, he quotes wagenknecht as an *authority* —on how to steal money from a newspaper for work not done   see the snideness of the incompetent:

> If we accept the bold statement on jacket and title page, The Recognitions is a novel. Further than that we can hardly go, but we can add that it must weigh four or five pounds.* The type is quite clear and a vague impression lingers that the characters, or some of them, are engaged in the arts; but what the story is about and what the problems and fates of these people are we have no idea. (*toronto globe & mail*)

in *the recognitions* (p936) the man in the green wool shirt meets his friend the stubby poet in a tailor shop, where theyre both having their flies fixed:

---

*2 pounds 7 ounces

6

And then they silenced, each bending forth, closer and closer, to
fix the book the other was carrying with a look of myopic recognition.
—You reading that? both asked at once, withdrawing in surprise.
—No. I'm just reviewing it, said the taller one, hunching back in
his green wool shirt. —A lousy twenty-five bucks. It'll take me the
whole evening tonight. You didn't buy it, did you? Christ, at that
price? Who the hell do they think's going to pay that much just for a
novel. Christ, I could have given it to you, all I need is the jacket
blurb to write the review.
It was in fact quite a thick book. A pattern of bold elegance, the
lettering on the dust wrapper stood forth in stark configurations of
red and black to intimate the origin of design. (For some crotchety
reason there was no picture of the author looking pensive sucking
a pipe, sans gêne with a cigarette, sang-froid with no necktie,
plastered across the back.)*

ie, the book to be reviewed is *the recognitions* itself   "all i need is
the jacket blurb to write the review"—obviously a satiric exaggeration

FIRE the *louisville courier-journal* hack for taking every bit of his
"review" from the jacket   theres not a sign he opened the book.
his plagiarism runs 6 lines, headline: Short Shrift

louisville courier-journal (in its entirety)	book jacket of *the* *recognitions* (excerpts)
The author attempts to give a full-scale portrait of our world today as he sees it: a chaotic world filled with hypocrisy, forgery, deception and hate.	THE RECOGNITIONS is a novel about forgery. In it William Gaddis has attempted a full-scale portrait of our chaotic contemporary world, in all its hypocrisy and lack of love
Scores of characters move back and forth from New York to New England, to Madrid, and other places,	background ranges from New York and New England to a monastery outside Madrid. Scores of characters move back and forth within the design, each one busy in pursuing his own desired deception.
all of them lost souls (!)	These and other damned souls
wandering about seeking security that continually eludes them.	(Mr. Pivner) is looking for security in the comforting columns of the daily press.
It is similar in many respects to Joyce's "Ulysses."	(backjacket quote, stuart gilbert): long though it is, even longer than "Ulysses," the interest, like that of Joyce's masterpiece and for very similar reasons, is brilliantly maintained throughout.

stealing a *moderate amount* from the jacket blurb is common practice
in the profession & therefore, im told, i must consider it ethical.

*in reference to all quotations from it in this and other articles in *newspaper, The*
Recognitions is copyright, 1952, 1955, by William Gaddis.

but it is not quite kosher to steal part of the review from the blurb and some of the rest from the associated press syndicate   here is the review from the *st louis globe-democrat,* written, according to them, by francis a klein:

klein 3/13/55 (in toto)	rogers review, ap syndicate (for publication 3/10/55); or ap's "author of the week" (for week of 3/7/55) blurb of *the recognitions*
A major writer pops over the horizon with this first novel that could well be a credit to a man with dozens in back of him. It is a big, hefty, sprawling (some 956 pages), involved in structure, realistic, and filled with an immense collection of odd bits of learning. The latter is sometimes appropriate, often not; one frequently needs to clear away the undergrowth to get at the tale. This has to do with forgery, emotional, spiritual and actual, which weaves in and out of this immense canvas that stretches from New York to Spain and back again.	(beginning of rogers review): Here is a major novel lards it with vast learning (from the blurb): The pattern of forgery, emotional and spiritual as well as actual, reappears again and again in the immense design of this novel, whose background ranges from New York and New England to a monastery outside Madrid.
The central character, Wyatt Gwyon, twisted and deformed by modern science, forges Old Masters;	faces of one central character. Their son Wyatt, tested by modern science and distorted and twisted by it, becomes a forger of Old Masters. (blurb): The central figure, Wyatt, is a painter who forges Old Masters
other people, other things, in a pattern that twists and turns, that is intensely dramatic and that repays the physical labor of turning 900 pages when 300 would have been sufficient. Mr. Gaddis worked six years on this book, but has not yet acquired the art of compression. When he does, his work will challenge that of any top creative artist of our time.	keeps it lean and strong with drama. a book to which he's given about six years (end of rogers review): with it, Gaddis assumes his place among our top creative writers.

theres not a word in kleins review that would have required "the physical labor of turning 900 pages" or 300 or 1   the *globe-democrat* subscribes to ap   proof that klein stole from rogers review is rogers "distorted and twisted" "by modern science" which klein uses

8

as "twisted and deformed by modern science"   this is a boner of
rogers if it means "crippled" (see episode starting p41 in *the recognitions*)   or if rogers meant it in an extremely general sense its still a
highly eccentric comment which klein could hardly have written
independently   & the beginnings and ends of rogers & kleins reviews
are almost identical

FIRE the thief klein, then   if klein had labored to turn the 900 pages
(all at once) to the *back* flap of the blurb he would have read, "*The
Recognitions* is not a work of realism in the accepted sense of the
term" & wouldnt have called the book "realistic"   but his plagiarisms
are both from the front flap

if you note the modifications klein made in rogers enthusiastic review
to be more "balanced" & cautious   & that klein quite possibly modi-
fied without having read any of the book except the blurb, you will
know what colossal nerve is

im biased for reviewers who favored *the recognitions* except some
who write like cold oatmeal   & this weird one who couldnt possibly
have read the book   stars . . . and embraces . . .

THE BOOKS PILE IN and some few stand up like stars in a Spring
sky. Embrace "The Recognitions" (Harcourt Brace) by William Gaddis as a novel in a thousand. It is a big, strong, well-written
American story peopled with reality and driven with a sardonic
dream that keeps the reader on edge all the way.

thats the whole notice   FIRE charles a wagner from his tabloid or
retire him to the astronomy column   what the devil does he mean by
"peopled with reality"?   and "driven with a sardonic dream"!

more important than these conmen   tho advance copies were sent
out months before review date* (powell)   I think less than ¼ of the
critics read *the recognitions* more than once   1 reading of this book
is not enough   especially not a hasty careless one   from mary
eugenia parke's review:

These remarks are the preamble to a cautious preliminary recon-
naisance of a monstrous and fascinating novel called "The Recognitions" by William Gaddis, whose first published work it is. Now it is
not impossible to read 956 pages intelligently in the space of a
couple of weeks. A dogged attack would get you through "Sironia,
Texas," for example, in that time without serious danger of laming
your brain. But "The Recognitions" is no "Sironia," and a proper
reading and evaluation would take several months, not weeks.
     My first impression is

who cares what it is! $$$$ why *not* take several months?   parkes
last para is remarkable, not really joking but sort of thrown out offhand
& to be forgotten:

On second thought maybe I am in the class with Wyatt, Basil
Valentine, Mr. Sinisterra. This review is probably a forgery too.

---

*anyway a competent review months after publication date is better than a
review appearing efficiently on the right date in the right column of the right
page in the wrong words

9

she took a couple of weeks not the several months needed, her
mediocre review *is* a forgery   from glendy dawedeit's review:

> This painstaking organization seems, even on first reading, to be
> one of the novelist's most positive achievements.

this & her preceding para are good   unlike most of the skimreaders
who being preprogramed have to guess that a "long novel" which is a
"first novel" must by definition be "undisciplined" & "sprawling"   but
the current cliches about "ambitious novels" & "erudite novels" lead
her astray:

> one flat statement about the book can be made with confidence:
> Entertainment is not a primary objective.

a bad guess, *the recognitions* being one of the most entertaining
books ever written   shes bound to guess wrong more often than
right since she didnt read it enough   certainly her guess that otto, in
the book, may be modeled after gaddis is amateurish & ridiculous

> More than one reading will be required for any fair estimate of such
> ornate and discursive language. Tentatively, however, one must
> credit Gaddis with some remarkable imagery as well as some
> meaningless rhetoric.

for "Tentatively," read "Incorrectly"   shes faking now   she plays it
safe, doesnt fail to find a balanced phrase but theres no safety for the
lazy & incompetent   she guessed wrong again, theres no meaning-
less rhetoric in gaddis' extremely careful writing

> To weigh the virtues of so massive a work with any finality would
> require longer acquaintance.

so   by necessity   her verdict is cautious, noncommittal which
means she underrates the book   what shows the rotten state of the
review racket is shes not at all afraid to say openly she didnt work
long enough to do her job   drs & lawyers underwork too but they
wouldnt dare admit it

the *nation's* cricket goes her one better   for the highbrow market
the pseudoprofessional thing to do is fake up a theme, a *structure.*
the theme should be as irrelevant to the book being reviewed as the
critics Originality can make it   whatever nonsense is dragged into
the 1st paragraph must return triumphantly in the last   john berger
impudently exploits "I only read it once" *as the fake theme*   exposi-
tion:

> BECAUSE I happen to be reviewing this 950-page novel I wish that
> I had time to read it again. But if I were reading it for my own
> interest I certainly would not do so. This fact demonstrates how
> specialized our cultural judgments have become, how far removed
> from our personal, comparatively spontaneous recognitions of what
> is good and bad. I think that Mr. Gaddis himself would agree with
> this. His title, "The Recognitions," is probably meant to be taken on
> several levels, but at least one of the themes of this book is the
> falseness, the obliqueness, of the type of recognition gained by
> artists in Western society.

this lecture on the conflict between desire & work isnt to the point.
the job berger took on was to read the book enough to write a competent review   his "dollar bill" & "ernest hemingway" boners (later)
prove he didnt   *thats* the point   he had earned the right to say
the following in print, & *only* the following: "i didnt read the book
enough to write a competent review of it—my guess is, it wouldnt be
worth the trouble"

how much would he have been paid for *that?*   or he could have
forgotten the paycheck & turned the job over to someone who was
willing to do it   an honest man would do one of the two, but a
critic—never!

what berger chose was to fake up a recapitulation for the last paragraph:

> This book has no vision because the writer can see no way out of
> the vicious environment he describes so obsessively. The facts are
> piled up because they may contain a clue to the way out—but he
> does not find it. The book lacks perspective both socially and
> psychologically. And in the end it is this, I think, that explains the
> awkwardness of the style in which much of it is written and its
> inordinate length. Because the writer is trapped, he barely en-
> visages the existence of the reader; unlike that of James Joyce his
> prose is unoral, heavy, silent; unlike a great but lengthy writer like
> Thomas Mann he has no desire to convince by accumulation; one
> finds oneself after nearly 1,000 pages in exactly the same place as
> one started. It is perhaps for that reason that I began by saying that
> I felt I ought to read this book again.

is the last sentence-and-a-quarter left over perhaps from some old
review of *finnegans wake?*   how crooked the last sentence is!

this time its the "constructive solution" cliche   a dirty one, perfected
in the days when communists dominated reviewing in the u s &
england   the perfect meeting of moscow & hollywood   give me
happy endings! im so miserable!   what cowardice   what if there *is*
no "way out" except to die   for 1000s of years countless ways out
have been peddled & we're no better off than before—the hydrogen
bomb proves that

but according to berger its easy!   any good novelist finds "the way
out," right in the last chapter   the bad novelist gropes around, but
somehow he cant locate it   of course berger means a *fake* way out.
he wants a writer to be a professional liar, not an artist

a writer can arrange for his characters to have relatively happy mo-
ments on the last page—but why should he?

mcalister read *the recognitions* twice & it was on hayes' "night table
for the past two months"   ive no proof, maybe most of the others
read much & carefully   theyre too modest to say so, or write as if
they did   it isnt that the review outlets cant pay overtime   they
spend large sums on all those thousands of routine reviews of routine
books   if they gave a good goddamn theyd spend a little extra on
the *real* job of reviewing   to see that great books are bought *now*
& not, like *the recognitions* will be, years & years after publication

because its reviews were faked   if the typists at a publishers
make a steady living, why not the great artists he publishes?

so, extra pay for extra time to review the books that need it   hows
that for a constructive solution   trouble is, the critics would use the
time for just one purpose: to make their counterfeits harder to detect

the notetaking trick   for the 4th part of a dollar i offer complete
instructions how to become a bookreviewer   its easy to sell a review
after just 1 careless reading of the book   a simple trick probably
used by most of the *recognitions* reviewers   you skim along confused, bewildered but you keep right on taking notes on any scattered
points that occur to your scattered brain   after "finishing" the book,
the notes   no matter how incoherent   can always be connected
up somehow   read the blurb again   refer to your numbered list of
cliches & guess which ones apply   then write it up good in jargon &
remember, your readers havent read the book either

and now, its boner time!

errors of fact, not of judgment   almost ½ the reviewers made 1 or
more   mr highet: *the recognitions* was published in 1955, not 1954.
mr hartman & kirkus service: it has 956 pages, not 965 or 946   mr
demarest: it cost $7.50 hardcover, not $5.00   mr north: it was published by Harcourt, Brace—not Harcourt, Bruce   mr yeiser: a chapter
appeared in *New World Writing,* not *New Writing*   livingston & north:
characters in it are named Feasley, Feddle, Valentine—not Feasly,
Feedle, Valentino   mr o'hearn: the book is called *The Recognitions,*
not *The Perceptions*   mr dolbier: it was written by William Gaddis,
not William Gibson   of course these are *all* printers errors

blunders will happen, especially when you hate your work   as the
3d paragraph of the 1st page of *the recognitions* says, aunt may is the
reverend gwyon's aunt, not wyatt's (boner made by corrington, livingston, smith, snyder, stevens, *time,* & wharton)   some skim the 1st
page, some the last   the book ends in fenestrula, not rome (laycock).
wyatt is not, at the end of the book, in a spanish monastery (corrington)   nor does gwyon become "more pagan than Christian" there
(smith)   wyatts childhood illness is not "recurrent" (simak)   the
"recent corpse" (simak) that sinisterra forges a mummy from is of the
little cross-eyed girl, murdered some 40 years before   to be sure,
this is "recent" compared to a genuine mummy

even these not-too-unnatural boners are not the kind you might make
after 1 reasonably attentive reading (tho they may seem similar in
content), but are the result of slipshod reading

FIRE dawn powell of the *ny post*   shes the champion careless slob.
(1) heracles is a barbary ape, not a barbados ape   (2) wyatt (not
someone else as powell implies) uses fresh hens eggs to make
tempera, not the "griffin egg" (a coconut)   (3) re sinisterra smuggling
his "hand-made mummy over the Spanish border as his mother"—he
takes it from "san zwingli" to madrid   both places are in spain   (4)
he hasnt yet made the corpse into a mummy when he takes it to
madrid   he could hardly pass off an egyptian mummy as his mother.
(5) esme takes heroin, but is not a "dope-pusher"   (6) it is herschel

who was described as a "latent heterosexual," not the blond boy
quoted in powells nexttolast para   (7) her last 2 quotes are not "At a
New York party" and "some place else" but both at the same ny party

frances burnette: "Greenwich Village where most of the action (that is,
talk) takes place"   about 140 pp in *the recognitions* are in greenwich village, or 15%*   as the boners get worse its no longer a
question of inaccuracy, carelessness   its again that the critics dont
do the job theyre paid for, they dont read the whole book with even a
minimum of attention   of course most of the *recognitions* reviewers
are mediocre untalented people   even doing their best they couldnt
produce an interesting review of a great novel on publication date.
they cant tell a great novel from an ordinary one, or they prefer the
ordinary   but they dont even try to do a good job   they fake it, &
the result is *amateurish* and *incompetent*—the 2 words that describe
the review racket

take ellington white's boner about the goat   he says when wyatt is
sick as a child, gwyon

    sacrifices a goat in whose blood he then bathes Wyatt with the
    result that, miraculously, Wyatt survives

its the notetaking trick!   browsing thru p41-54, white noted that
gwyon was reading a passage in frazer that mentions the sacrifice of a
goat (p49)   he forgot to read the next 2 pp where a *barbary ape* is
sacrificed &   (p51) wyatts shoulders are blood-spotted from his
fathers hands, but he is not "bathed in blood" & its not a ritual action.
or berger:

    There are many secondary and subsidiary characters— . . . a
    counterfeiter of dollar bills

imagine berger scurrying down p489, taking a quick note on the 1st
half of a sentence:

    That was two hundred and fifty one-dollar bills,

& not even reading the rest of the sentence:

    bleached to print the twenties on.

(sinisterra speaking)   sinisterra would be offended, as a craftsman,
at being called a counterfeiter of dollar bills, that is, an amateur.
where was berger for all the other pages where the counterfeit twen-
ties are mentioned over & over & over   this berger who made such a
condescending big deal about he "ought to read this book again"—did
he read it even once?   in any real sense of the word?

FIRE the bastard!   another of bergers subsidiary characters:

    a man who either is or pretends to be Ernest Hemingway.

cautious like a critic!   but if berger had paid the least attention to
the Big Unshaven Man in *the recognitions* how could he have

---

*when do i get my honorary litt d?

imagined the B.U.M. to be even conceivably the real ernest hemingway?

—Is that really Ernest Hemingway over there? someone said as they entered. —Where? —Over there at the bar, that big guy, he needs a shave, see? he's thanking that man for a drink, see him?

There was a yelp from the end of the bar; and a few, who suspected it of being inhuman, turned to see a dachshund on a tight leash recover its hind end from a cuspidor. The Big Unshaven Man stepped aside. —I'm God-damned sorry, he said. —Oh, said the boy on the other end of the leash, —Mister Hemingway, could I buy you a drink? You are Ernest Hemingway aren't you?
—My friends call me Ernie, said the Big Unshaven Man, and turning to the bar, —a double martini, boy.

The beard at Otto's table said, —Is that Hemingway? Ed Feasley looked over at the Big Unshaven Man, who had just said, —No queer in history ever produced great art. Feasley looked vague, but said, —There's something familiar about him.

Otto and Ed Feasley, with Esme between them, moved toward the door. The Big Unshaven Man turned away when Feasley passed. —Of course I know him. A damn fine painter, Mr. Memling, he was saying, as he took a quart flask out of his pocket. —Would you mind filling this up with martinis? Yes, what you read about me is true, I like to have some with me. Sure, I'll look at your novel any time, he finished, as the boy handed a ten-dollar bill across the bar.
—I sure as Chrahst know him from somewhere, Feasley said.
—That's because he's Ernest Hemingway, said a voice nearby.

—Say, is that really Ernest Hemingway behind me?
—What if it is, what would that make you?
—He, I . . . I'd like to meet him, I think he's a great writer.

—Mister Hemingway? My name is George . . .
—Glad to see you, George, said the Big Unshaven Man. —What are we drinking?

—Damn fine music, Mozart, said the Big Unshaven Man. He had just finished making a whole pitcher of martinis [from the hostess's liquor at a cocktail party], which he poured into a large pocket flask. —I tell you true.

—Hemingway? Well he said he's staying at the Ritz, but I say the Ritz was torn down simply years ago . . .

And down the bar, the Big Unshaven Man was offered a job writing the lonely-hearts column for a newspaper in Buffalo.

(the recognitions p306 307-8 309 310 525 525 632 641 749) hemingway was a lousy writer, but he never came on like that!

stevens hadnt read the long sections on the deighs, or how could he write:

Mrs. Deigh, the literary agent who resembled, from behind, an uneven stack of sofa cushions

14

the literary agent being agnes deigh & the stack of sofa cushions, her
mother   its the notetaking trick—stevens built his review from the
blurb & hardly glanced at the book

FIRE edward a bloom for forgetting to read large chunks of the book &
not faking up his notes right:

> The chief symbol of despair is Wyatt Gwyon, who has been reared
> in the image of sin imposed by a New England Calvinistic aunt. His
> father, a Protestant minister, is secretly attracted to the ritual of a
> kind of Primitive Catholicism.

wyatt isnt a symbol of despair   only a stupid man with a mind full of
inflexible cliches could think so   now bloom could make this kind of
"judgment boner" even if he read the book every page   the "Primi-
tive Catholicism" tho, ive got the goods on him   theres many pages
on the reverend gwyons mithraism in *the recognitions*—some of the
crucial scenes hinge on it—even the most stupid reader couldnt help
learning that mithraism is not christian   re mithra, bloom isnt a
stupid reader hes a *non*reader   he skipped all the passages except
one   &, by bad luck, he picked the wrong one, where aunt may
makes the same mistake he does:

> —And this? she appeared one morning in the study door poised
> rigid, dangling forth a pamphlet between forefinger and opposable
> thumb, —tell me how *this* got among *my* things? As though there
> might have been movement in the air, the pamphlet fluttered open,
> quaking its suspended title: *Breve Guida della Basilica di San
> Clemente.* In his chair, Gwyon startled, to reach for it, but stayed
> held at bay by her unpliant arm, and unyielding eyes which had
> fixed the distance between them. With a single shudder he freed
> his own eyes from hers and fixed them on the pamphlet, to realize
> that it was indeed not being offered in return but rather in evidence:
> not an instant of her stringent apparition suggested surrender.
> —Another souvenir from Spain! she accused, a page headed in bold
> face *La Basilica Sotterranea Dedicata alla memoria di S Clemente
> Papa e Martire* fled under her thumb. —Pictures of Spanish idols, . . .
> fragments of Byzantine fresco captioned *Nostra Signora col Gesù
> Bambino* almost caught her attention, —Catholic images . . . Another
> page fell over from the hand quivering at her arm's length, and
> bringing her foot a step past the sill she held it out that space
> closer to him; nothing moved. But the sill's sharp creak underfoot
> penetrated, a signal for her to hurl it at him, or down; for him to leap
> and snatch it. But nothing moved until she retired recovering her
> advance, and spoke with bitter calm, looking square at the thing,
> —A nice . . . place of worship! The illustration pinioned by her gaze
> was captioned *Il Tempio di Mitra.** —Look at it! a dirty little under-
> ground cave, no place to kneel or even sit down, unless you could
> call this broken stone bench a pew? She got her breath when he
> interposed, —But . . . —And the altar! look at it, look at the picture
> on it, a man . . . god? and it looks like a bull!
>   —Yes, a pagan temple, they've excavated and found the basilica
> of Saint Clement was built right over a temple where worshipers
> of . . .
>   —Pagan indeed! And I suppose you couldn't resist setting foot
> inside yourself? Did you? Again she paused, getting breath she

---

*italian for *The Temple of Mithra*

appeared to prepare requital for his answer, admission or denial, and when he withdrew mumbling only —Set foot inside myself . . . ? she snapped immediately, —At least I have finally had the satisfaction of hearing you call the Roman Catholic Church *pagan!* She filled her grievous gaze a moment longer with the picture, and finishing with —Now that we all know what the inside of a Catholic church looks like, . . . she was gone, holding the abhorrent memento at arm's length, her eyes alert upon it, as though it might take life and strike.

(p37-8)   bloom made exactly the same kind of notetaking slip *twice.* he wrote:

Mr. Pivner is a narcotics addict.

on 34 pages of *the recognitions* that bloom skipped, mr pivner appears solo   he owns a hypodermic needle, but hes not a narcotics addict, hes a *diabetic*   bloom couldnt have read one section about pivner without realizing this   & again, the 1 passage he did read, he got wrong   rushing thru p521 he jotted down a quick false note from—

—I could sue you for false arrest, Mr. Pivner said when he got into the lobby, with a policeman, —if that would do any good. Do you know what you've done?
Behind him the policeman talked with the tall bellboy, who said, —Well Jesus, *I* thought he was drunk. The guy with him was. The policeman said, —We got him down to the station house and found a needle on him. We thought he was a junkie. He's real pissed-off.

FIRE anne fremantle of *commonweal* for building her review on a boner   fremantle uses the "sophisticated but sincere" variety of critic-style   she wears a wry flippant mask, its supposed to hide a depth shes too civilized to more than hint at   the result is insufferably cute:

But when Mr. Gaddis tries too hard, as in several of the Yirrupean scenes, he fails by overreaching.

But that which we must go without is, above all, our own false image of ourselves, that false face of perfection which leads us, like methane, along the primrose path you know where.

where?   to h-ll?   how easy these modern religious get to believe their own sacré words are profane!   fremantles styles a 2dorder counterfeit, at heart she *is* flippant, superficial, cant stand honesty or depth, has to snipe   heres the condescending "x, very x" trick:

Mr. Gaddis is angry, very angry with the world as he finds it

according to this cheap trick the "angry, very angry" target isnt really angry only pretending   the cheap trickster is supposed to be the sincere one*   fremantles main points are religious   example:

Wyatt's father, a minister of a First Congregational Church in New England, who buries his wife in Spain, turns to Mithraism. Indeed, the author seems to accord Mithraism a respect he refuses to its

---

*cheap trick because it tries to cut anger—all feeling—down to size

16

successor. (ie, to christianity)

can such things be?   impossible!   personally my credo is, the
christians succeeded in murdering all the mithraists & that proves
xianity is the true religion and the religion of love

> It is not possible to come to a Christian conclusion, as Mr.
> Gaddis does, without starting from a Christian premise: and that
> premise must be, alas, the Fall, and that we are all Jacob, and must
> learn to live with our falsely furry faces and fingers, and like it;
> and accept the Redemption that we are only given because (and when)
> we admit that we do everything badly. (fremantle)

but *does* gaddis come to a christian conclusion?   & if so, what is it?
her cliche assumption is that the concluding parts of a book must be
conclusive, represent what the writer *really* thinks   but this is only
true of writers who have to fake an end because their book never had
any middle   *the recognitions* has an antiending, eg the main character walks away on p900 & is not seen again   the last page, where an
artist is killed by the completion of his work, sounds one of the main
(nonchristian) themes of the book—but so does every other page

per fremantles orthodox view   expressed in a style more suitable for
an uncle wiggily story   a christian conclusion must be based on
mans imperfectibility, original sin   she must believe that gaddis
christian conclusion either agrees with hers   or more likely she
thinks gaddis thinks we can & should stop sinning & become perfect.
shes wrong either way   the "last word," for what its worth is in the
last scene where wyatt appears, especially his speech on p896 (the
last quote from him in issue #10)   he says he wont try to become
perfect but will "live it through"   in fremantles terms, he says that
deliberate sin is correct action (& leads to redemption?)   according
to fremantles church this is an antichristian conclusion

but thats only ½ the joke   her christian conclusion misjudgment is
built on a scene at p900 of *the recognitions* which she calls the "final
conversion scene"   what a farcical blunder!—especially for such a
"knowing" critic   based on a stupid, careless misreading

> The final conversion scene, where in a mirror, the face of one
> "having, or about to have, or at the very least valiantly fighting off, a
> religious experience" is seen, suffers from its echo, or hint, or
> possible recollection, of similar paragraphs in *Marius the Epicurean,*
> Henry James, Lytton Strachey and "The Journey of the Magi."
> (fremantle)

an impressive list!   how politely & kindly she accuses him of plagiarism!   only—it isnt a conversion scene at all   its a joke   ludy,
a phony writer of religious inspirational stuff, is visiting à spanish
monastery to get "material":

> He was a comfortable man of middle age, dressed in an expensive
> suit of Irish thorn-proof, the last two buttons of the vest undone, or
> rather, never done up at all, in token of the casual assurance he
> afforded himself as a novelist successful enough to be referred to
> by his publishers as distinguished. At this moment he wore an
> expression of intent vacancy, his face that of a man having, or
> about to have, or at the very least sincerely trying to provoke, a

religious experience: so it appeared to him, at any rate, when he
passed the mirror and confirmed it.
   He stood now, staring down at a boy poised on the balustrade of
the church porch below, a boy big enough for the Boy Scouts, con-
stricting his person to see how long a stream he could send out
into the muddy plaza, where a sow and three pigs were passing in a
dignified procession of domesticity. The distinguished novelist
stared, to see, he was bound to admit to himself afterward, if the
stream would reach, when a bird flew up against the glass square
before his face, and continued to flutter there as he staggered back
and almost lost his balance on the bricks of the floor. He recovered,
returned the length of his room, and sat down on the bed. Notes for
the magazine piece he'd begun lay on the table beside him. He saw
them there and looked away. The moment of religious experience
was gone again. The boy directing his stream from the very porch
of the church had upset it; the bird had dispatched it. The distinguished novelist clasped his hands between his knees, and
wondered if it were a mealtime.

(p857-8)   later ludys terrified in a scene where wyatt holds a bird in
his hand & ludy thinks wyatts going to kill it   & now   in the "final
conversion scene"   ludy gets back to his room & finds a bird *in* it—

and though he tried frantically to chase it toward the front, toward
the windows and out, it fluttered the more frantically from one
picture to the other, and back across the room and back, as he
passed the mirror himself in both directions, where he might have
glimpsed the face of a man having, or about to have, or at the very
least valiantly fighting off, a religious experience.

the 2 parallel passages express one of gaddis themes, of substance &
accident   that those who live by vanity may receive from accident
the unwelcome gift of becoming what they pretend to be   (cf otto's
sling)   ludy, distressed by the accident of the bird being in his room,
takes on an expression like the one he faked when not distressed

from hate to indifference

take a quantity of critics insults   chop off qualifying & balancing
clauses—often designed to strengthen insults (by pretending objec-
tivity) not mitigate them   cut out somewhat, almost, rather, seems,
sometimes, at times, a certain amount, in other phases, in some
respects   *the recognitions,* then, is appalling, awkward, arrogant, no
work of art   it is baffling, and a Bore   confused & confusing.
cruel, claustrophobic, a literary curiosity   dont buy it—its debasing,
demoralizing, diabolical, has no decency   or if this excites your
lower nature, its also dull difficult dreary—& disgusting   evil, but
exasperating   a fatuous foul-mouthed formless failure!   inchoate,
incoherent, shows immaturity & lacks imagination   & kindness.
murky muddy monstrous   nihilistic   an overwritten oddity, obscene
& obscure   profane & pretentious   repulsive or repelling   scur-
rilous-scatological, sneering-snarling-sprawling-squalling, says north of
the *ny world telegram & sun*   and adds, has no trace of sincerity.
an uncontrolled exhibition   no vision   wearisome*

---

*key numbers 40-4-53&63-4 8-56 82-55 84-4-54&63 35-35-53-53 75-55-9-
35&53 53-53&63&66 46-53-63-3&28&30&62 46-62-3-4 53 85-8&50-55&63

18

as for gaddis personally, he "lacks judgment" & his self-love is "embar-
rassingly apparent"   hes a cynic with a narrow jaundiced view and a
depraved mind*

just some words of welcome to americas best writer   where does all
this hate come from   everybody knows, for centuries its been said a
critics an envious man   theyre always supposed to have got over it
a generation ago but they never do   critics only concern with im-
mortality, if he was immortal he too could write a great novel someday.
if a million critics were strumming on a million typewriters . . .

how is hate hidden   anger shades down to contempt, contempt to
condescension & innuendo, then "balanced" with a little sting left, then
complete indifference   which, toward greatness, is not unlike hate

anger   FIRE sterling north for flipping over the wrong book, for
moralizing instead of reviewing:

> an evil book, a scurrilous book, a profane book, a scatological book
> and an exasperating book.

> What this sprawling, squalling overwritten book needs above all is
> to have its mouth washed out with lye soap. It reeks of decay and
> filth and perversion

> Nowhere in this whole disgusting book is there a trace of kindness
> or sincerity or simple decency.

norths stupidsquare review is based on the naive hope that its gaddis
who made "all love, all learning, all science, all art and all religion
counterfeit" & not us   (disregarding the "all"s)   norths own values
appear in 2 interesting lists:

> It is a sneering, snarling, foul-mouthed attack on Protestantism,
> Catholicism, modern medicine, the "middle-class" virtues, repre-
> sentational art, our economic system, our educational system,
> motherhood, fatherhood, sympathy, faith, devotion, birth, death, art
> criticism, literary cr[i]ticism, sobriety and any other form of balance
> or order that you can name.
>
> * * *
>
> It is also, and with more reason, an attack upon abstract art,
> homosexuality, the moral and physical filth of some parts of New
> York's Greenwich Village, the posturing of the Left Bank in Paris,
> the stupidity and futility of Bohemianism, the disgusting aspects of
> drug addiction and alcoholism, the illiteracy and corruption of
> Central America, the bigotry of Spain, the simple-minded violence of
> Hemingway, the complex and intentional obfuscations of Gertrude
> Stein, the latent witch-burning tendencies still vestigial in New
> England, and self-love (so embarrassingly apparent in every sen-
> tence the author writes).

only 3 of these 29 themes do not appear in the book & only about 7
more are grossly misleading

---

46 6&53-36-35-50&55&63 53-9&21&38&74 53-84 all 53 53 63 4 35   see
bibliography for reviews #s refer to

*key #s 35-53 17&18&35&69-63-53

contempt the hate is still there, even uglier but the critic makes it appear that he personally is not angry   like the *new yorker* quote (again):

> this novel challenges the reader to compare it with Joyce's "Ulysses." So challenged, the reader is obliged to say that while Mr. Gaddis has been very brave, Shem the Penman has won the day.

(shem the penman: joyce, as selfparodied in *finnegans wake*)   "challenges" is part of the "ambitious" cliche   the implication is that when an artist does highly organized work, his sole intention is to challenge you, to force you against your will to tell him how great he is   its merely a cliche, a trick, because it can be used equally well against a phony or a real artist*   "obliged to say" testifies to the critic's coy reluctance to stab   more contempt:

> old Gaddis is a whiz with the reference cards in the library (bass)

> there is every indication that the author expects this work to fling itself directly into a class with, say, *Ulysses*—if not somewhat past that point. (hartman)

> not even Rupert Brooke [had] such a passion for putting in every Greek, Latin, German, French, Spanish, Italian, Yiddish and four-letter word he knows, Oh, Salvation, how many yawns do we suffer in thy name. (fremantle)

"Salvation" is fremantles christian-conclusion boner again   "angry, very angry" is like the "dim view" trick:

> By implication [Wyatt] represents the plight of all modern artists, in Mr. Gaddis's dim view of things, if not the corruption of all levels of modern society from the television industry to the lower depths. (geismar)

> "The Recognitions" abounds with prototypes of Greenwich Village, circa 1920, whose nebulous stream-of-consciousness speech often becomes lucid enough to uncover the author's dim view of things (livingston)

> He sees no virtue in anything and, indeed, the novel is itself a fantasy embroidered and overwhelmed with elaborate symbols and too many fine and despairing phrases. (smith)

the "dim view" trick is designed to smother feeling in cliche   only 2draters use it   it means "im afraid hes angry, he disapproves. maybe hes angry at me!   im afraid   but presto, its not so serious, he only—ha ha!—takes a 'dim view'   whew, back on familiar ground. i dont really care, you dont care, so *he* doesnt care   saved!"

he doesnt care, hes just "vastly disturbed":

> Mr. Gaddis is vastly disturbed by the obscene, the immoral, the sacrilegious. (laycock)

wrong again, laycock!   & dawn powell again, master of boners,

---

*anger or sarcasm would be ok vs a bad book, but not tricks & masks

20

master of contempt:

A Genius, a Bore, or Both

—a typical snotty *ny post* headline   & typical of that *liberal* newspaper's smoldering hate for anyone who excels

   Seven-fifty for a book without art, maps, recipes or even tele-
phone numbers? Why? And how was a young, unarmed writer able
to slug a publisher into even reading such a vast tome, let alone
publishing it? To claim they give you 956 pages of novel in return
for your money is like offering you a giant headache in return for
your aspirin.

   And some place else someone asks, "What are you supposed to be,
an honest man just because you don't have a necktie?"

                              * * *

   Is "The Recognitions" supposed to be an honest novel because it
has no quotation marks?

powells just having goodnatured innocent fun   her last innuendo is
false analogy: in *the recognitions,* the man in the green wool shirt (who
the question is asked to) *does* think not having a necktie makes him
honest   powell anyway likes to throw in dirty wisecracks at random,
just for the hell of it or because she cant think of anything else to say

FIRE rochelle girson for rank presumption   selfimportance   fills a
column about how she had 2 ideas about gaddis & they were wrong

   Dark suspicions have been voiced in industry circles lately that
William Gaddis must have at least partially subsidized the publishing of his mammoth first novel, "The Recognitions." Else how could
Harcourt, Brace (or any other firm) have afforded to bring out a 956-
page book by a completely unknown author? (The fact that it is
tagged $7.50 by no means insures the gamble.) So, not being an
especially bashful sort, we upped and asked them.
   No, they said emphatically, the novel was not subsidized. Reason
for the risk: "We feel that Mr. Gaddis is an important writer."

shes lying about the "industry circles," reputable publishers dont
publish subsidy novels   you can see its ridiculous if a 1st novel or a
long novel is subsidized by the author   & equally ridiculous if it isnt

   Mr. Gaddis, she said, works at nothing but his writing, and this is
the first time the 32-year-old author has had anything published.
Then he must be rich, we put in slyly. Wherewithal is a fact of life,
and it takes leisure to amass that young man's erudition. Again no.
Mr. Gaddis lives on Long Island, where his sole income is from a
house that he and his mother rent for something like $50 a month.
Largely self-educated, he has lived "in rather desperate circumstances" in order to get "The Recognitions" written, his editor told
us, adding firmly, "we believe in the book very much."

the editor's remarks are wasted on miss poisonpen   whose financial
& educational report is all wet   a rich writer is ridiculous, while a
writer "starving in a garret" is ridiculous   ridicule the universal
solvent, appropriate for any art or any artist   the only thing not

ridiculous is Position—to be a hack journalist spinning out a column of zero   "slyly"

condescension   contempt with the spite diluted but the fake superiority retained:

> It is a pity that, in his first novel, he did not have stronger editorial guidance than is apparent in the book—for he *can* write very well— even though most of the time he just lets his pen run on. (kirkus)

> Gaddis is a cynic but he's young. (desbarats)

> A literary event, of sorts. (*newsweek*)

> the polysyllables, sentence fragments and foreign words give the novel too "arty" a tone. Sometimes these devices are effective. But please, Mr. Gaddis, not through all 956 pages. (dixon)

> But Please, Mr. Gaddis, (dixon headline)

as wyatt says to recktall brown, "You are so damned familiar."

> Mr. Gaddis is in the modern tradition of pronoun misplacers whose leader is another William, the man from Mississippi, Faulkner. (laycock)

> Occasionally this author shows some depth or perception; and he apparently can manage a narrative. And if, please God, this book is not a "success," he may meet up with some human beings whom he can use as characters. Then perhaps he will really write. (hill)

"human beings" instead of "the odd offshoots of our society" who "have filthy minds and foul mouths"

> WHAT THEN are we left with at the end of this novel besides tired eyes, an unchallenged brain and a feeling of frustration? The book is large but the scope is small so the comparison with Joyce is out. The author's wit, irony and erudition we will grant. We will not yield on rich diversity, however, and we must point out a certain amount of immaturity.
> And we cannot agree* that Gaddis has surpassed Eliot in the delineation of the Waste Land. Rather, like the streets in Prufrock, this novel leads you like a tedious argument of insidious intent to an overwhelming question:
> Is the book at least a magnificent failure?
> And we must reply that there is nothing magnificent about it. And we go back to rereading Joyce's "Ulysses" for the umpteenth time. (bass)

the pygmy condescends to the giant   FIRE bass, dixon, hill, and the kirkus *newsweek* & *new yorker* hacks, for delusions of grandeur

innuendo   like bass again:

> SOMETIMES a novel is more of a physical than a mental challenge.

---

*with the stuart gilbert quote (back of *recognitions* book jacket)

or harrison smith, president of the influential *saturday review* (his
syndicated review appeared in various newspapers but not in the *sr*
itself where the review, even worse, was by maxwell geismar):

> His story is not difficult to penetrate. But, aside from his obvious
> dislike of the complexities and crassness of the modern world, it
> may be interpreted in more than one way. Would Gaddis prefer the
> harshness and brutality of medieval Spain, or the bloody and ruth-
> less tyranny of Rome under Tiberius, to life in a 20th-century
> democracy? His novel seems to give an affirmative answer.

that is, *perhaps* gaddis *might seem to be* a reactionary & a fascist!
the stupidest of all the paragraphs the critics wrote about *the recognitions,* well, one of the stupidest   the book happens to give a
definite negative answer to smiths pussyfooting question   he should
spend more time reading the books he reviews, & less hiring scum to
write typical *saturday review* articles about whether, perhaps, thomas
wolfe drove his editor to his death & whether, perhaps, *ulysses* is a
hoax   boss smith, go fire yourself!

a quote from *the recognitions* (p9-10):

> The Real Monasterio de Nuestra Señora de la Otra Vez had been
> finished in the fourteenth century by an order since extinguished.
> Its sense of guilt was so great, and measures of atonement so
> stringent, that those who came through alive were a source of
> embarrassment to lax groups of religious who coddled themselves
> with occasional food and sleep. When the great monastery was
> finished, with turreted walls, parapets, crenelations, machicolations,
> bartizans, a harrowing variety of domes and spires in staggering
> Romanesque, Byzantine effulgence, and Gothic run riot in mul-
> lioned windows, window tracings, and an immense rose window
> whose foliations were so elaborate that it was never furnished with
> glass, the brothers were brought forth and tried for heresy. *Homoi-
> ousian,* or *Homoousian,* that was the question. It had been settled
> one thousand years before when, at Nicæa, the fate of the Christian
> church hung on a diphthong: Homoousian, meaning of *one* sub-
> stance. The brothers in faraway Estremadura had missed the
> Nicæan Creed, busy out of doors as they were, or up to their eyes
> in cold water, and they had never heard of Arius. They chose Homoi-
> ousian, of *like* substance, as a happier word than its tubular alterna-
> tive (no one gave them a chance at Heteroousian), and were forth-
> with put into quiet dungeons which proved such havens of self-
> indulgence, unfurnished with any means of vexing the natural
> processes, that they died of very shame, unable even to summon
> such pornographic phantasms as had kept Saint Anthony rattling in
> the desert (for to tell the truth none of these excellent fellows knew
> for certain what a woman looked like, and each could, without
> divinely inspired effort, banish that image enhanced by centuries of
> currency among them, in which She watched All with inflamed eyes
> fixed in the substantial antennae on Her chest). Their citadel passed
> from one group to another, until accommodating Franciscans
> accepted it to store their humble accumulation of generations of
> charity. These moved in, encumbered by pearl-encrusted robes,
> crowns too heavy for the human brow with the weight of precious
> stones, and white linen for the table service.
>   They had used the place well. Here, Brother Ambrosio had been
> put under an iron pot (he was still there) for refusing to go out and
> beg for his brethren. There was the spot where Abbot Shekinah (a

convert) had set up his remarkable still. There was the cell where Fr. Eulalio, a thriving lunatic of eighty-six who was castigating himself for unchristian pride at having all the vowels in his name, and greatly revered for his continuous weeping, went blind in an ecstasy of such howling proportions that his canonization was assured. He was surnamed Epiclantos, 'weeping so much,' and the quicklime he had been rubbing into his eyes was put back into the garden where it belonged. And there, in the granary, was the place where an abbot, a bishop, and a bumblebee . . . but there are miracles of such wondrous proportions that they must be kept, guarded from ears so wanting in grace that disbelief blooms into ridicule.

did you read those pages, boss smith?   do they show a preference for "the harsness and brutality of medieval Spain," as you so pompously put it?   dont they show something much worse, a refusal to think & write in the terms of your conventional, 1-dimensional mode of consciousness?   & your "bloody and ruthless tyranny" of tiberian rome, dont you ever get tired of your own stale prose?   try a refresher course, take a 1st glance at p512-3 ("Among Rome's earlier and more cheerfully dealt contributions to the decline of civilization" . . .) or pp245, 256, 386-7:

—We live in Rome, he says, turning his face to the room again, —Caligula's Rome, with a new circus of vulgar bestialized suffering in the newspapers every morning.

(p386, basil valentine speaking)   of course we dont live in rome but in a "20th-century democracy"   but if a country with a   theoretically   decent system of government cant live decently, isnt it time to stop judging novels, faute de mieux, by their conforming   or not   to crude political slogans?   & valentine has the bad taste, instead of demanding the extension of socialsecurity benefits, to speak of the "masses, the fetid masses"   would adlai stevenson say a thing like that?   would jack kennedy?   did you know, boss smith, *the recognitions* callously, undemocratically refuses to take a stand on atombomb tests, civil rights, public housing?   gaddis didnt write one sentence that would be *fit* to appear in a *saturday review* editorial. why pull your punches—hes worse than a fascist, hes an artist!

indifference   theres so much of this i hardly know where to begin. take 1 subject, comparison of gaddis with other writers   shouldnt the critics know something about gaddis' work before they start playing the comparison game?   but they cant wait, heres some quotes shading down from anger to indifference:

He rambles on and on, needlessly and even disgustingly, striving ineffectually to do in 956 big pages what Evelyn Waugh accomplishes in less than 200 small ones. (hill)

He takes a smack at everything and everybody in the manner of Eliot and Joyce and Cummings, but they do it much better and much, much shorter. (bass)

to date the one valid criticism of Wolfe is his lack of discipline. In comparison with Gaddis, Wolfe wore a literary strait-jacket. (simak)

There is also a good deal of the newsreel technique which Dos

Passos used in "U. S. A." But is the fact that we can now add quotations from radio broadcasts to newspaper headlines adequate reason for doing this all over again? (wagenknecht)

The cocktail party that covers pages 568 to 646 should be required reading for all foreigners who really wish to understand the American way of life; it is first-rate reporting, and out-Hemingways Caldwell. (fremantle)

is this world of weirdies any less real than a world of Willis Waydes? At least, they are antidotes for each other. That is why this is the book I would take with me to Suburbia. (powell)

Dostoevsky, with his intellect multiplied by a factor of ten, but without a soul. (hartman)

if Mr. Gaddis has failed to bring off his first attempt to write our Dunciad, it is not inconceivable that he may in a later work succeed. (*u s quarterly book review*)

perhaps as disconcerting in its own way as "Ulysses" or "Finnegan's (sic) Wake" (bloom)

The style is a tumbling together of Wolfe and Joyce, of raucous laughter and sentimental tenderness, of satire and objective seriousness. The novel laughs (or weeps?) at Greenwich Village, at advertising, at Americans abroad, at organized religion, at false dentures and illness. It is melodrama and gothic horror. It is grotesque and overwritten, but above all it is terribly earnest and by no means to be dismissed. (bloom)

the last few quotes are mostly "balanced"   reader: answer yes or no. bloom: yes or no   his lush synthetic prose is a fine example of "criticstyle" at its worst

price's prediction was wrong:

this is a tale that will be widely read, and one that will engender considerable opinion, very little of it temperate. Anger over the work will be great, and it will find forceful expression in many places.
I should not be surprised to learn soon that efforts will have been made to suppress it in various sections of the nation. Yet it will also find stout defenders.

½ the *recognitions* reviewers dont totally conceal their hate   most of the text of these, & all the text of most of the rest, play it safe   their indifference & torpor conceal a great distaste   not now for the best books only   critics are bored by their fakework, dont like any books. good books are a little more demanding, more fatiguing, thats all

couple of generations ago underpaid hack reviewers took it out in destructive power like any prison screw or socialworker   now they dont dare, dont care   the change even in the last 20 years is remarkable   instead of north's moralistic kind of attack, the *recognitions* reviews are mostly dull, dogged attempts to do a hack job not worth doing   as "they" expect the critic to do it   death replacing evil

but dead reviews are more dangerous to a great novel than vicious
ones   you used to be able to find the best books by reading the
reviews   the most hated books were the best   now its harder.
sometimes you can sense the critic working against his own resistance
to convince you   especially by what he tacitly assumes   that a
novel is really quite ordinary tho a bit eccentric   of medium interest,
nothing to get excited about   thats the book to read!   like this:

long stretches of "Ulysses," even in a first puzzled reading, were
felt to be the work of genius. "The Recognitions"—or that part of it
that is understandable—is no more than very talented or highly
ingenious or, on another level, rather amusing. (granville hicks, in
the *new york times*)

but often you cant tell at all, because the critic has read so carelessly
that he doesnt know even unconsciously what kind of book it is.
soon reviews will be no help at all

& wordofmouth, that depends on whose mouth   its not only the
market, the audience thats been broadened for the sole benefit of the
exploiters of art & pseudoart   but still more disastrously, the avantgarde   every asst copywriter who owns a hifi & refuses to read the
reader's digest thinks hes hip to the latest but hes not

the recognitions had less to gain from a major new york publisher in
1955 than *ulysses* from an amateur publisher (a paris avantgarde
bookstore) in 1922   gaddis was indifferently reviewed, neglected by
an indifferent public   both enthusiasm & backfiring anger having
become oldfashioned   conditions for the success of this kind of
great novel havent improved

ulysses was banned as obscene in the u s & england for over a
decade   subject of evil comments from the most reputable critics.
but there were always enough enthusiasts, enough "crazy joyceans"
from the avantgarde to keep the book from being forgotten, assure its
eventual success   where are the enthusiasts now?   where are
the people who should have been writing, pushing *the recognitions*
long ago?   even if im wrong about its greatness, where are they
pushing some other neglected work?

i suspect part of it comes from bringing democratic ideals into judgment of art where they dont belong   art is more like a jungle, in a
jungle the animals dont have equal rights   writing a poem with good
intentions doesnt make you a dylan thomas & doesnt mean you should
be published 50% of the time & him 50%   & ive seen plenty of
avantgarde magazines run just that way, with a list of the editors
friends as a pleasant substitute for picking the manuscripts out of a
hat   & the complaint about publishing "names"   its true when
work from "names" is accepted without reading it, as often in effect it
is   but usually the reason wm burroughs is published & ------ ------
isnt, is that ------ ------ cant write worth shit!   & why be afraid your own
work will be scorned if you admit someone elses is better?   beckett
was a "crazy joycean" & it doesnt seem to have harmed him

i say to the avantgarde, dont abdicate!   part of our work has always
been pushing neglected masterpieces & if we retire to contemplate
our clippings we cant be replaced   by who, the academics, the

reviewers?   *playboy* & the tv hippies cant do it, all they have is taste.
they dont *care*, so they cant do it   but you can

FIRE granville hicks   his *new york times* review tried to destroy a
great novel   a review built on innuendo & projection

i learned what bastards like hicks are in ayn rand's *the fountainhead.*
hes a real ellsworth toohey except he doesnt always know what hes
doing   he should read *the fountainhead* & become an iago instead
of a worm   his review starts:

> WHAT we have here is certainly a puzzle and perhaps a challenge.

the "balanced" statement again!   *book review digest* fell for hicks
tricks, rated his review noncommittal   its not noncommittal to say a
books *certainly* something bad & *perhaps* something that looks good
but will turn out to be only "ambitious"

> William Gaddis (among other things, to be sure) is playing a game
> with such readers as he may be fortunate enough to have, a game
> for which he has devised the rules.

in 1955 hicks could affect how many readers gaddis would "be fortu-
nate enough to have" but his times running out   except for demanding 10% of the gross for a plus review, hicks & the other *recognitions*
reviewer-hacks did a great job of making its satires prophecies   in
the recognitions crémer, an artcritic refused a bribe by wyatt, reviews
him down (p74):

> —Archaïque, dur comme la pierre, dérivé, sans cœur, sans sympa-
> thie, sans vie, enfin, un esprit de la mort sans l'espoir de la Résur-
> rection.

("Archaic, hard as rock, derivative, without heart, without sympathy,
without life, in a word, a spirit of death without the hope of Resurrection")   many years later crémers comment on valentine's forgery of
a forgery is (p665):

> —Un sacrilège, ce visage-là, archaïque, dur comme la pierre,
> voyez vous, sans chaleur, sans cœur, sans sympathie, sans vie . . .
> en un mot, la mort, vous savez, sans espoir de Résurrection.

("A sacrilege, that face, archaic, hard as rock, you see, without warmth,
without heart, without sympathy, without life . . . in a word, death, you
know, without hope of Resurrection")   it seems he always uses the
same blast (or the favorable gem on p663)   monsieur hicks fulfills
the word of the prophet:

hicks reviewing gaddis	hicks reviewing paul goodman (4 yrs later)
playing a game with such readers as he may be fortunate enough to have, *a game for which he has devised the rules.*	the book is difficult in an arbitrary fashion, full of *games of which Goodman has invented the rules,* full of recondite allusions and private jokes, full of self-conscious sophistication.

(italics added)   his gaddis review continues:

It is part of his game to conceal the identity of his characters in many scenes: the hero's name, for instance, is not mentioned for hundreds of pages, and other characters can be recognized only if one remembers a ring or a coat or a trick of speech. It is part of his game to use six or eight languages and to overwhelm the reader with his knowledge of Flemish painting or early church history, or medicine. He hints at parallels with the patristic literature, creates a complicated pattern of father-and-son relations, and, by introducing well-known persons, gives the impression that he is writing a *roman à clef.*

what "well-known persons"?   its bergers "ernest hemingway" boner again   or is it some other character or beast in *the recognitions*— the ex-army pilot named charles dickens, the faggot writer named buster brown?   basil valentine, the reverend gilbert sullivan, albert & victoria hall, hadrian, heracles, popeye, doctor fell?

roman à clef!   as hicks says in *the living novel* (1957 p222):

What are we to make of a reviewer (in *Partisan Review*) who . . . attempts to evaluate C. P. Snow's *Homecoming* without having read any of the other novels in the series of which it is part, a series he preposterously characterizes as a *Bildungsroman?* (my dots)

now, the innuendo that gaddis "game" is "to overwhelm the reader with his knowledge"   its the erudition cliche   hicks pretends hes forgotten the artistic relation of 20thcentury techniques to the novels theyre in   he judges the techniques in isolation as something pasted on & unnecessary   but eg the question&answer chapter in *ulysses* has an artistic purpose, to show dedalus & bloom from another angle, in another light that cant be supplied by conventional dialog & description   a novel is *not* a work of nonfiction   if joyce introduces the subject of parallax the purpose isnt to show off joyces knowledge of astronomy

gaddis doesnt use techniques for their own sake either   wyatt & others often arent identified in dialog because their "tricks of speech" (& what they say!) identifies them sufficiently   the principle of economy: being identified by the context, adding a "Wyatt said" would weaken the identification (by overdoing it) not strengthen it   other times the name of the character may not spring to mind at 1st reading, its for "timegrowth"   on rereading, the novel doesnt remain static but changes as the previously unrecognized is recognized   which, by changing the timerelation of the reader to the book, also changes the dimension of time *in* the book   its "world" can be experienced as a whole as well as part by part

likewise "early church history" isnt in *the recognitions* for its own sake (but to throw a different light on the religion or irreligion of the characters) & the "complicated pattern of father-and-son relations" isnt there for complications sake any more than the patterns of jealousy are in proust   of course if a woman is to wear dozens of fancy costumes she should look striking to begin with   gaddis characters can carry any amount of overlay but i wouldnt advise hicks to dress up the poor creatures of his own soporific novels in more than their workaday clothes   but if he'll stop projecting his inability to transcend the ordinary onto better writers by accusing them of using nonfiction techniques for nonfiction purposes & just to show off   and if he'll get close enough to *the recognitions*   (with or without "effort" but definitely with more than "a first puzzled reading")   to see the book as it is, he might try imagining if it would really be improved by (1) adding a thousand "Wyatt said"s (2) cutting out all the furrin words (3) no church history, refer only to characters lives at the moment (4) no more than 2 father-son relations (5) cut out luxuries like mr "pott" & "dick" who tho they dont represent the "well-known persons" whittaker chambers & dick nixon, have a humorous relation to them

hicks continues:

Clearly there is more here than one reading will reveal,

—did he or didnt he?—

and the question is whether the more is worth the effort.

the "difficult" cliche   writing above kindergarten level strews malicious landmines in your path, you thread thru with great "effort" & no reward   poetry should be translated to *ny times*style so you get the literal meaning without difficulty   critics prefer the same old unchallenging mush   they get no pleasure from reading so they prefer anesthesia to the choice between pleasure & pain

The reader thinks, as Mr. Gaddis obviously thought, of Joyce's "Ulysses."

guess again—gaddis read 40p of *ulysses* in college, period!*   honest critic might say influence from *ulysses* possible—joyce & gaddis in some ways have similar attitudes, as a result some of their technical resources resemble   but the innuendo of plagiarism in "as Mr. Gaddis obviously thought" is dishonest   the same kind of projection as "ostentatiously" in hicks last para

When that book was read soon after publication, before a body of criticism had smoothed away the difficulties, there was much in it that was mystifying and no small amount that seemed deliberate mystification.

but joyce beat the rap!   hicks loves projection—anything in a novel that looks different *could* be error & error *could* be "deliberate" malice. since every good novel contains something unusual every good writer can be personally attacked & thats just what hicks wants

"smoothed away the difficulties" is a revolting phrase   joyce cant be persuaded to write down to the critics level so rewrite him from outside, by encirclement   tho whats really difficult is to read *ulysses* after reading a dozen asinine books about it, books whose only life is in the quotes from joyce

But what one remembers is that long stretches of "Ulysses," even in a first puzzled reading,

---

*"Perhaps without 'Ulysses' Gaddis' novel could not have been written" (parke)

—did he or didnt he?—   who cares what "one" remembers from a
1st puzzled reading!   as hicks the idealist wrote in *the living novel:*

> spokesmen for the people who want to eat their cake and have it
> too, who are smart enough to recognize the shoddiness of the
> blatantly commercial novel but too indolent or too distracted to
> come to terms with the genuinely serious novel.

(218)   & as hicks the idealist wrote in a 1956 *new leader* review:

> When a literary journalist comes upon a good novel, his first obliga-
> tion is to say so. Afterward he can try to explain why it is good and,
> if he sees fit, why it is not so good as it conceivably might be.
> These are important matters, but they are not so important as that
> an act of creation has taken place.

(quoted in *living novel* 177-8)   heres hicks idealism in practice:

> But what one remembers is that long stretches of "Ulysses," even
> in a first puzzled reading, were felt to be the work of genius. "The
> Recognitions"—or that part of it that is understandable*—is no
> more than very talented or highly ingenious or, on another level,
> rather amusing.

what a hypocrite!   *only* "very talented"—what condescension!   for
centuries the great work of one generations used to beat the next
with, how can this still fool anyone?

hicks malice with "balancing" again   the pluses shrink to insigifi-
cance, the minuses are monstrously swollen   while whetting the
knife for a sharp close he spends a para describing *the recognitions*
contents   of course in 68 words he cant do it   then the clincher:

> The novel is full of episodes that, in a less ambitious work, one
> would be happy to call promising. Indeed, it is only because Mr.
> Gaddis, in his first published work, has so ostentatiously aimed at
> writing a masterpiece—and has made upon his readers demands
> that only a masterpiece could adequately reward—that one is dis-
> satisfied.

how evil can you get?   he admits *the recognitions* is "very talented"
but his whole review from the 1st key word "puzzle" to the last "dis-
satisfied" is meant to discourage readers from buying it   yes, hes
always ready to welcome a 1st novel thats promising, *unless the
promise is fulfilled*   talent not yet fulfilled can be helped as an
equal, doesnt threaten him   but he stomps on fulfilled talent that
needs his help only as his superior   hicks the idealist has this dirty
side too (*the living novel* viii)   hes refuting critics who confuse the
ravages of their own middle age with "the death of the novel":

> there have never been so many serious novelists at work in America
> as there are in this period; I am not talking about great novelists,
> who are rare enough in any age,** but about men and women who
> believe in the novel, who write out of themselves and not for the
> market, who recognize that there is a craft to be mastered and are

---

*in a 1st puzzled reading?

**not as rare as youd like!

30

determined to master it, and who have already made it clear that
they have talent enough to warrant their ambitions.

everyone has enough "talent"   the problem is the work produced.
talent is only what gives a critic or publisher a cheap thrill when he
takes you to lunch the 1st time   each literary parasite once hoped
to be a real writer, was determined to master his craft & ambitious to
do good work   then he failed & became a critic or editor   the
writers he loves havent yet got further than he did, but might   but if
they already have he hates them   the whole publishing racket shares
hicks fatal flaw   prizes are for promise that may never be fulfilled,
not for the impoverished one whose 6th books very good but no better
than his 5th

equally important, *the recognitions is* a masterpiece   writing a snotty
review like hicks vs gaddis automatically disqualifies you as a critic
forever   recognizing masterpieces is *the* job of the critic—not writing competent reviews of the unimportant   poor hicks, having a
masterpiece sneak up on him with no warning, no previous "body of
criticism" to tip him off!

hicks, who i must admit never misses a chance to expose himself as a
fraud, really screwed the cap on in a review of paul goodman's *the
empire city* (1959):

> there is something a little phony about this attack on phoniness. I
> remember a comparable book that appeared a few years ago, an
> ambitious, difficult, bitter book, William Gaddis's "The Recognitions."
> I felt that "The Recognitions" was a failure but that it was an honor-
> able failure, the failure of a man who had aimed too high. By com-
> parison Goodman seems to me to play it safe, to use all the tricks
> of the advance guard without venturing very far out in front.

thats not what he said 4 yrs earlier!   a man whos "so ostentatiously
aimed at writing a masterpiece" & failed makes a *dis*honorable failure
not an honorable one   give hicks another 4 yrs & he'll twist it around
again to be favorable enough to go in his collected critical works without disgracing him   maybe he should try "dishonorable success" 1st
just in case

the *ny times* has shown   with a really comparable book   that it is
indeed "happy" to praise "less ambitious work"   its jay williams'
novel *the forger,* reviewed by another enemy of art, orville prescott (6/
12/61)

*the forger*s a novel about young ny painters, one of them forges a
painting in the manner of giorgione   it covers much the same sub-
ject-matter as a large part of *the recognitions*   like gaddis, williams
has "flash" (flashy in the good sense), his novel is competent but lacks
depth   its attitude, pointofview, center is that of an ordinary person,
or rather the stereotype of an ordinary person ("maughams flaw"), not
of an individual person as in great novels   williams characters are
only moderately "there"   compare the parallel characters adrienne-
esme, rufus-wyatt, beechley-recktall brown, von reimar-valentine,
donald-stanley, youll see the difference   prescott says:

> Now, in "The Forger," he has written his best novel so far, a novel

that is a psychologically interesting personal story and also an
intimately authoritative guided tour of the special world of contemporary art in New York City.

prescotts whole review of an ordinary novel encourages the potential
reader as hicks discouraged him from reading a great one   thats the
ny times for you, past present & future

back to hicks review   the editors of the worst bookreview section in
the world postscripted it with a note showing hes *not* one of those
critics who cant write a book themselves:

> Mr. Hicks is the author of "There Was a Man in Our Town" and
> other novels.

"one" has unearthed a review of this very novel!*   reviewer's putting
questions with ending questionmarks instead of indirectly & his failure
to use enough passive verbforms stamp him as an amateur who has
failed to master criticstyle, but here it is anyway:

> Granville Hicks' *There Was a Man in Our Town* (New York: Viking
> Press, 1952) is the most forgettable novel I've ever read.
> On the elementary-technical level the book is competent. But
> competence only makes a dull book monotonous.
> Mr. Hicks' characters arouse my compassion and engage my
> sympathies. Like all characters in fiction they are denied the privi-
> lege of existence in real life: this makes it doubly unfair that they
> are denied any real existence *in* the novel. You can tell them apart,
> but they are "flat." They have that fatal "guy-down-the-block-who-I-
> don't-know-very-well" quality, the vague humdrumness that is the
> sure sign of the secondrate novel. They lack self-generating force &
> have to be pushed around by the plot.
> The book is not insensitive to pressing social needs. It is a
> political novel, the story of a crusade—gallant though for the mo-
> ment thwarted—to improve the politics of a small New England
> town by a factor of about one-half of 1 percent.
> It is no negativistical novel, but rings a note of wry and wary pro-
> fessional optimism. Nothing is Pollyanna-perfect: the characters
> suffer, but not nearly as much as you would expect from their
> circumstances. The author has supplied them with the equivalent of
> bulletproof windows for every emotional contingency.
> The book is not without moments of deep philosophy and the
> tragic view of life. As the narrator remarks (p. 270): "Nonsense. Do
> you know the saddest sentence in the English language? It's 'You
> can't eat your cake and have it too.' Because that's what everybody
> wants to do, and since it's impossible nobody can be happy for long
> at a time."
> Mr. Hicks never exploits the pornographic. His novel treats sex
> strictly as a prime causative factor in interpersonal relations.
> He hates children and presents them always as unprovoked
> aggressors, tormenting adults who ask only to be left alone. Or he
> does *not* hate children and is merely—and may one suggest, a little
> ostentatiously—striving to be "different."
> Why was this novel written! It can't be for money: dull books don't
> sell. Or fame: the goddess is notoriously indifferent to candidates in
> neutral gear. Or for its own sake: why bother? I keep getting the
> strange idea that Mr. Hicks *is not a novelist at all*. I mean this

---

*not from the *ny times* or *saturday review*, which were plus

literally: he has some quite different profession.
Imagine a golf-mad steel corporation in Pittsburgh. All the executives must join the country club and play golf. The ambitious young men try to shoot in the 70's; no one complains about the president's score of 150. But the mass of executives had better play in the 90's—not too good, not too bad. Similarly, in Mr. Hicks' real job it is required that he write a novel once in a while, out of office hours. Not a very bad novel, certainly not a very good one or of real value to anyone including himself, but just "a novel." Every few years he must grind one out: his employers don't read it, but they feel reassured by its existence.
But what kind of job does he have?

FIRE maxwell geismar for his stupid *saturday review* review   built on the "strawman" trick   like fremantle's & livingston's its procrustean. he starts with a corny reprise of "it cant be that good":

IN SOME quarters of the literary scene today William Gaddis's novel "The Recognitions" is bound to be praised to the skies, and this reviewer keeps wondering who is being taken in.

me!   geismars review is creative   he doesnt understand *the recognitions* at all, so he invents another *recognitions* all his own:

A New England minister has buried his wife in Spain, and he slowly becomes converted not to the Christian mode of salvation, but to the ancient pagan rituals of propitiation and sacrifice. This is actually an underlying theme of the novel—that we have lost not only belief today, but the primary sense of pleasure and biological functioning in life which the ancients had.* Robert Graves, for example, has developed this theme in a series of brilliant historical novels.

im voting for "pleasure and biological functioning" too this year, but its *not* a theme of *the recognitions*   what, say, pagan religion & alchemy had over modern religiosity & chemistry is given as substance, significance, *emotional* passion   the book is not especially sensuous & its attitude toward pleasure as such is indifferent, skeptical, mocking. & by the by, why would a christian minister be expected to be *converted* to "the Christian mode of salvation"

my guess is, geismar already had that graves para in mind & stuck it onto the 1st book that might seem relevant   if the guest doesnt fit the bed—tough!   & he tops it off with the strawman trick   in his last para   having projected his own views wrongly onto gaddis. he blames gaddis for not living up to them:

"The Recognitions" never achieves any kind of contact, not merely with modern life, but even with the biological vitality which it stresses.

which it does *not* stress   john w aldridge   writing in 1956 that "*The Recognitions* received indifferent to stupid notice in the leading New York literary supplements"   suggested the reason might be

---

*or as plagiarized by o'hearn a week later: "The thesis seems to be that belief has vanished from modern life and with it all joy and creativity"

"most of the reviewers have never grown beyond the view which was fashionable in the 1920s"   which makes a neat contrast to geismars absurd idea that *the recognitions* itself "is really a typical art novel of the 1920s"

And the fatal flaw of this genre is simply that the central figures, as in Mr. Gaddis's case too, are only half-artists,

does geismar really believe that failures by characters *in* a novel are failures *of* a novel?

who never really engage our sympathy or interest; who never represent anything but themselves.

figures like Joyce or Picasso do engage our sympathy when they break through traditional forms of art.

sure they do—a generation later!   "engage our sympathy" is the compassion cliche, the rotting ulcer of american criticism today   "or interest"!—when *the recognitions* is an accepted masterpiece, if anyone tries to claim geismar was a competent critic those 2 words will disprove it

The outside world of modern American life, which is surely a legitimate subject for the novelist today,

thats deep thinking, geismar!

is described so imperfectly, and so superficially as to make us feel that the novelist himself has never known it.
    It is quite possible that Mr. Gaddis is not even pretending to an elementary realism,*

"quite possible"—of course he isnt!   if geismar doesnt get the book why doesnt he look it up in the blurb? ("*The Recognitions* is not a work of realism in the accepted sense of the term")   with masterly confusion geismar takes the criticisms a fool might make of novels not totally realistic   & implies theyre faults peculiar to *the recognitions*

since the plot is complete fantasy,** somewhat reminiscent of Rex Warner's "Wild Goose Chase."

the plot doesnt resemble *the wild goose chase* in the least!   is there no limit to what these hacks will drag in to fill space?

But if people as people no longer concern this new school of symbolists or surrealists—

was kafka unconcerned with "people as people"?   is it only realism that presents reality?

which can be an indictment either of modern life or of them—then we must still be caught up not merely by the craft of the artist, but by the central vision of life.

---

*o'hearn: "This book makes no pretense to realism"

**its not   the fantasys imposed on a realistic ground—the opposite of what warner does

the "vision" cliche!   an artists weltanschauung has no artistic meaning in itself but has to be transcended if not redeemed by "the craft of
the artist"   like beethoven redeeming schillers inane doggerel in the
9th symphony, or bach redeeming christ   but to the hack critic
artists beliefs are more important than their work—& a lot easier to
write about!   "he says man is essentially good, so his work must be
essentially good"   its like the *ny posts* ½assed sportscolumnists:
hitting a lot of homeruns is small pickings compared to The Question:
when the fans throw sodabottles at the star does he show "maturity" &
"humility"?   ℞ for critics: the vision cliche with equal parts of
moralistic cant, sniping at their superiors & not having to work hard

geismars review could have been written without reading the book, to
which it has little relation   he concludes:

> Whatever is of genuine merit in the novel is drained off into a
> continuous verbal vaporizing; and whatever is here of genuine
> talent is consumed by an obsession, as I can only call it, with
> pretentiousness.

conform! (punctuationwise)

critics are so conformist that the least unusuality   even of mere
punctuation   gets struck at like a rattlesnake

(yes i *know* youve heard all about conformity madisonavenue & indi-
viduality & you dont want to read another word about topics stale
usedup & newly unfashionable   which means: youve been conned
again!   when an idea starts to look dangerous to Them they destroy
it with the novelty trick   they grab onto it themselves & write it up
everywhere & everyphonyway   until you get sick of it, the novelty
wears off, the ideas not dangerous but passe & meantime the right
people have made plenty money out of it   especially compared to
what theyd make if they wrote about their own ideas   but ideas
arent like hats   1 fashions not replaceable by another except among
the fashionable timekillers   "conformism"s just as important before
during & after the henry luce boys get the hots for it)

the critics know not how to stop those mad fools who   hidden off in
a corner somewhere   make weird offensive experiments with punctuation   critics set up the barricade at the entrance to the mass
market, ie their own reviews

youd think 30 yrs after *ulysses* they could stand for dashes used in
dialog   but no:

> an "experimental" flavor which requires such things as dashes
> instead of quotation marks (hartman)

at 1st an innovation is absurd unnecessary, used just to show off   if
it takes root its "experimental"   if its growing, claim the noveltys
worn off, its passe   if it takes over, languish for the good old days.
purpose of the barricade: to keep english usage exactly as it is until it
withers   distinguished sciencefiction hack & reviewer simak says:

> To compound the entire situation, the author does not believe in

quotation marks. He is not new or alone in this, but while other writers who have avoided quotation marks as a mark of fuddy-duddyism have been careful to indicate where the marks would have been, Gaddis treats this matter of mechanics with the same high disdain as he does the matter of clarity in other respects.

not true!   theres not one para in *the recognitions* where its not clear whats dialog & what isnt   the dash is looser less efficient than quotemarks cause theres no closing dash & contentdevices must be used to separate conversation from narrative that follows it in the same para   but writings not engineering & the most efficient techni-cal device isnt always the best one   dealing with the "unnecessary" formal problem of talk-narrative border enriches the book   (since it can be dealt with, & more than dealt with, in so many ways)

the recognitions also menaces linguistic stagnation by use of a great deal of ellipsis in dialog   i havent seen this used before for the same purposes   startling result, the dots make it possible to charac-terize in new sharp ways   the critics react not to the function but merely to the novelty   angrily:

lapses into insulting half-finished sentences (north)

or psychosomaticly:

endless portentous gasping conversations which read as though the author had his thumb on the windpipe of each speaker (swados)

the dialogs not like that at all   north snorts, swados chokes because the characters dont always get neatly to the end of their sentences like in most novels, nor do the sentences necessarily end as the char-acters planned

the same panic & reactive anger underlie highet's more selfcontrolled version:

he makes several of his chief personages so incoherent that their speeches are often incomplete; he is the master of . . . of the . . . the dots. . . .

very funny!   to smash the "experimental" without exposing fear & rage, if Authority has no access to impersonal punitive action then try humor:

Is "The Recognitions" supposed to be an honest novel because it has no quotation marks? (powell)

highets "incoherent" is wrong   wyatt has more dots than anyone & is the most coherent character in the book   he always has some-thing definite he must say & he says it   niggling about dots doesnt change that fact

after reading section ii of *the recognitions* try the earlier draft printed in *new world writing*   it has less dots, as a result wyatt is much less sharply defined & his conversation is much less "there"

36

"unprintable"

> [An English publisher's readers] had no doubt of its moral purpose, since it criticises severely the life which it depicts. Nevertheless, because the book, for 2 per cent. of its total length, describes sexual incidents in coarse language, no printer could be found. (st john-stevas)

the anecdotes not true, secker & warburg being scared by poor u s sales not by the censors*   *the recognitions* doesnt describe sexual incidents for 20p or in coarse language   theyre described indirectly, as are most sensory experiences in the book   many of the shocking remarks in the caricature sections are about sex   on the whole, among novels of the 1950-60s the books relatively not sexcentered**. then why the "unprintable" bit?

> repetitious parade of erudition in the obscure and of the unprintable in word and deed (laycock, *boston globe*)

> a squad of persons whose deeds, like their words, are well-nigh unprintable. (*newsweek*)

> I should not be surprised to learn soon that efforts will have been made to suppress it in various sections of the nation. . . . language current only in a jail yard. (price, *cleveland press*   my ellipsis)

the recognitions can hardly be unprintable—it was printed   & has had no trouble with censors   what they mean is gaddis doesnt shirk words like fuck & shit when theyre needed   the *boston globe, news-week* & *cleveland press* can *never* print these words   idiocy & cowardice! as if their offices were on the 13th floor & they called it the 14th

its obscene *not* to print words like fuck & shit   & in lieu to print the Smirk   titterings about "four-letter words"—now theres a dirty word:

> a passion for putting in every Greek, Latin, German, French, Spanish, Italian, Yiddish and four-letter word he knows (fremantle)

or about promiscuity:

> a series of bohemian women who go to parties to get bed companions (berger)

massmediamen never tire of giggling over "four-letter words" & celebrities mistresses   (why dont they write about advertisers mistresses)   cant they see the Smirk isn't a criticism its a damaging confession about their own sexlives!   taking the role of the man who stays in the whorehouse parlor making knowing jokes & hoping noone will notice he never goes upstairs

or retreat to turnerism***:

---

the recognitions will be published in england this year [1962] by macgibbon & kee

**nor does it have "a Swiftian obsession with eliminative functions"   (wharton)

***term honoring the critic dr turner in wolfe's "portrait of a literary critic" (*the hills beyond* 152-3) who "first made the astonishing discovery that Sex is Dull"

It is weighed down also by too much lubricity, too many anecdotes of merely scandalous appeal, too many bad literary puns. (o'hearn)

but not everyone is weak-sophisticated, stern moralism continues:

> Most of these slimy citizens* are in some way connected with the arts and are undergoing psychoanalysis when not busy with public orgies, private orgies, conversational orgies, or other conspicuous displays of their alleged erudition and proud depravities. (north)

> The casual reader who is tempted to plunge into this work should face the logical question, "why bother?" Unless one belongs to the extremely small group of people who are satirized here, or has—and is willing deliberately to indulge—a morbid taste for obscenity, there is scarcely any answer to the question. (hill)

fortified by his s.j. & vow of chastity hill edges over from critic to censor:

> In the current moral atmosphere it may be asking too much of the average publisher to expect him to act with some sense of responsibility. It should be pointed out, however, that a book of this type does not merely cater to an already debased taste; it tends in itself to be debasing. Obviously the author does not intend to demoralize, but the tendency—however unconscious—of his work is an objective fact and one of which the publisher should be aware.

& his magazine lists *the recognitions* in *moral* class iv: "Not Recommended for Any Class of Reader"

blasphemy

as religion sickens the catholic church transforms itself increasingly into a secular moral-political party   thus the jesuit hill mounts a full-scale attack on gaddis "obscenity" but writes only 1 veiled reference to religion:

> What erudition the book contains—and it lays claim to much—seems to be largely reducible to the *Golden Bough* and a college course in comparative religion. Mr. Gaddis shows all the young cynic's naïveté in his willingness to believe any explanation of a phenomenon provided that the account be not traditional; if it should have an element of the disreputable, so much the better.

(no virginia, he does *not* welcome the novelist who at last quotes church fathers & stresses our catholic ancestral world   early church historys too disgraceful to bring out in the light   better to leave it in reverent obscurity)

yet religions a main theme of *the recognitions***   it contains no unusual amount of "obscenity" but much more than usual of blasphemy   (ie much more than zero!)   as some of anselms remarks:

---

*characters in *the recognitions*

**which makes for some surprising transformations of the reallife source   i lived in the greenwich village milieu of *the recognitions* in the early 50s & dont recall the subject of religion getting an hour a year

—If you think the Church wouldn't do an about-face on contracep-
tives if it owned a block of stock in Akron rubber! And how much
real estate do you think they own in this whorehouse of a world?

—I meant to tell you how glad I am about your play, Stanley said
to Otto. —I am, honestly.
—Thank you, I . . . I know you are, Otto said, and put a hand to his
shoulder. —You're really good, aren't you Stanley.
—I wish I were. I wish everyone was.
—There'd be a lot of crazy priests out of work. Work! Hahaha . . .
—Anselm, you . . .

—Do you know who I envy? I envy Tourette. He had a disease
named after him, a very God-damned rare one.
—Are you drunk? If you're not why don't you shut up.
—When you have Tourette's disease you go around repeating
dirty words all the time. Coprolalia. Everybody below Fourteenth
Street has coprolalia.

—I envy Doctor Hodgkin. Anselm was cleaning his teeth thought-
fully with a folded match cover. —He had a disease named after
him.
—What kind of disease?
—Hodgkin's disease, for Christ sake.

—You know who I envy? Anselm broke in on them impatiently.
—I envy Christ, he had a disease named after him. Hahaha, hey
Stanley?

(184, 531, 531, 533, 534)   after which anselm joins a monastery.
others in the book are religious antireligious or both   some are
merely religiose:

—How's your writing?
—Movie magazines, simply all sex, Herschel answered, making an
effort, —the most obvious perversions. I'm writing a whole series
now on movie stars and God. They're all exactly the same. They all
believe that *Some*thing is carrying us on *Some*where, and they
simply reek with the most exquisite sincerity.

The hole in the roof had, of course, been repaired; and the
interior done over in taupe and white. The gilded organ pipes had
disappeared; and so had all of the harsh angles of woodwork;
instead, eyes and voices were lifted to smooth turns and flexures
in taupe, and two bullet-shaped chromium lights trained on the
pulpit, whence the President of the United States was exhorted
with benedictions for the first time since the assassination of
James A. Garfield. The oaken boards, where hymn and verse had
been posted during services, were no longer necessary, for programs were now printed up every Sunday, detailing not only the
service but other church activities. The programs sometimes ran to
three or four pages, not counting the front which bore a "nice"
(slightly Gothicized) likeness of the church itself.
Sturdy brass basins had taken the place of the wicker baskets for
the offertory (not, in this illuminated Protestant world, of course, the
tendering of bread and wine for Divine approval before their con-
secration; but here, according to custom, that equally exquisite and
perhaps more realistically inspired moment of communion, when
"Dick" received the brimming basins from the ushers, and solemnly

held them up somewhere over his head in a gesture of intercourse of the most intimate dimensions imaginable to those who had contributed).

At the table to his left, an American Protestant minister in rimless glasses tasted Cinzano for the first time, made a wry face, and said, —It's just part of this big job we're all pulling together in. Do you know this new word, *Caprew* . . . ? It's made up of the first two letters of Catholic, Protestant, and . . .

The Pope himself (who had spent part of today blessing drivers at a motor-scooter festival, whom he praised for their "courage and agility") had, on another inspired occasion, received "silent and eloquent" messages from the "agitated sun," and witnessed "the life of the sun under the hand of Mary."

(180, 714-5, 909, 917)   gaddis narrative is never religiose: the relation of religious & antireligious is complex   in the 20thcentury world of *the recognitions* few love & those who do are not loved in return. the religious experiences are likewise incomplete, marred   true love & faith are defined by exclusion not by example

but the critics think in stereotypes   theyre religiose, believe in strict separation of church & life   their chief dogma, religion is to be Respected—neither mocked nor taken seriously   they know only 1 sort of religious novel: waugh-greene, the reformed cynic giving his readers a sermon because theyre still young & frisky   its o sancta simplicitas when gaddis subtleties collide with critics crude expectations   product: a maze of misinterpretations

north says *the recognitions* makes all religion counterfeit, is evil, scurrilous, profane, a sneering, snarling, foul-mouthed attack on protestantism & catholicism:

If I were so naive as to believe in the devil I would say that young Mr. Gaddis had willingly sold his soul to achieve this Faustian first novel.

& o'hearn: "negative, rebellious preoccupation with religious themes" "jejune blasphemies" (but "not necessarily . . . irreligious")   or, more unexpectedly:

Throughout the novel, there is a passionate preoccupation with religion (rolo)

or "Mr. Gaddis' novel, shrouded in mysticism" (mcalister)   or stanley "a religious fanatic" (fremantle) or anselm "in whom religious mania assumes the form of theatrical blasphemy" (rolo)   is joining a monastery "mania" is trying to live a christian life "fanaticism" is occupation with religion *pre*occupation?   as an atheist i can only envy the power of the religiose to destroy religion

then theres sleightofhand so "religion" means only "christianity":

he finds everyone corroded through the decline of love and the absence of Christian faith. (*time*)

so gwyon's "mad" because mithraist (stocking) and mithraism is "pagan

mumbo-jumbo" (bass)   better a makebelieve xian than a real pagan!
& gwyons last sermon, which is mithraist & doesnt mention xianity
"is the very embodiment of all anti-Christian mythology" (hartman)

since all religion is xian *the recognitions* must be medievalmad a la
anglocatholic ts eliot:

> Like ["The Waste Land"], it views the Middle Ages and the early
> days of the church as a time of spiritual, philosophic and even
> esthetic purity and our age as a cesspool of depraved and impotent
> souls. (rugoff)

guess again!   (see *recognitions* p9-10 quoted above, p22-3)   then
the book must be catholic antiprotestant of later date:

> the book's central conflict: Zwinglianism and Transubstantiation,*
> most exactly, or materialism vs. spirituality, reality vs. idealism, or
> bad vs. good. (mccarthy)

guess again!   then it must be protestant, hussite:

> Quite naturally, Mr. Gaddis suggests that the only cure lies in a
> return to the faith and love embodied in Christ and the church.
> Regrettably enough, however, he pictures religion as only a mockery
> today, either so dogmatic and demanding that it drives Gwyon's
> preacher-father to Mithra-worship and gin and his son to insanity, or
> so hypocritical and commercial that its churches become merely a
> curiosity for tourists and its art forms simply a source of revenue for
> imitators and manufacturers.
>   One can only suspect that the recurring mention of the religious
> reformer, John Huss, emerges as Mr. Gaddis' plea for a human
> being in this day and age willing to stand up for his beliefs, willing
> even to be burned at the stake for what he cherishes. And because
> there is no such man among the people of "The Recognitions" one
> is apt to hope that the author, in real life, may find and bring to light
> in a further novel this more positive individual who does exist—in
> the grass roots, if not the fleshpots, of America. (livingston, *dallas
> news*)

pretty stupid, huh?   in babylon i never dreamed the voters of dallas
texas were so eager to burn at the stake for jesus sake

the influence game

> Incidentally, I never could understand why every book of mine in-
> variably sends reviewers scurrying in search of more or less cele-
> brated names for the purpose of passionate comparison. During the
> last three decades they have hurled at me (to list but a few of these
> harmless missiles) Gogol, Tolstoevski, Joyce, Voltaire, Sade,
> Stendhal, Balzac, Byron, Bierbohm, Proust, Kleist, Makar Marinski,
> Mary McCarthy, Meredith (!), Cervantes, Charlie Chaplin, Baroness
> Murasaki, Pushkin, Ruskin, and even Sebastian Knight. (vladimir
> nabokov, foreword to *invitation to a beheading* 6)

---

*transubstantiation: bread & wine are bread & wine in accident, but christ in
substance   zwinglian: bread & wine are b&w in accident & substance, christ
only by contemplation of faith

names dropped about *the recognitions:* hieronymus bosch, breughel the elder, rupert brooke, erskine caldwell, joyce cary, céline, madison a cooper, ee cummings, salvador dali, dante, dickens, dos passos, dosto-yevsky, norman douglas, dreiser, ts eliot, augusta j evans, faulkner, fielding, flaubert, james frazer, egon friedell, gide, robert graves, hawthorne, hemingway, hogarth, aldous huxley, henry james, st john of the cross, joyce, juvenal, kafka, dh lawrence, wyndham lewis, malcolm lowry, thomas mann, pater, picasso, alexander pope, proust, ayn rand, walter scott, sterne, lytton strachey, swift, tolstoy, vergil, rex warner, evelyn waugh, nathanael west, thornton wilder & thomas wolfe

112 references to 53 names!   only a dozen of the 112 attain even the mediocre   90% are just playing the influence game   you cant say anything worth saying about joyce *and* proust in 1 offhand phrase   what does it mean to say gaddis "has some of Joyce Cary's breadth and exuberance"?   nothing!   demarest's just namedrop-ping to give his writeup a "literary tone"—the easy way   it fills a little space & *looks* like it says something   groups of names are even more obviously gratuitous:

reminiscent sometimes of Laurence Sterne, sometimes of James Joyce, and sometimes of Norman Douglas. (coldwell)

strange assortment of influences from Dickens to "The Fountain-head." (dawedeit)

an Evelyn Waugh-Thornton Wilder-Thomas Wolfe hybrid (mccarthy)

The style is a tumbling together of Wolfe and Joyce (bloom)

theres no such book!   the fakery can be judiciously quantified:

He has learned much from James Joyce and perhaps a little bit from D. H. Lawrence. (white)

or plucked from the blurb:

spiritual forebears are Joyce's *Ulysses,* Eliot's *The Waste Land,* and Gide's *The Counterfeiters.* (rolo)

ulysses & the waste land are featured on the jacketback of *the recog-nitions* & per the blurb its "a novel about forgery" & includes "an honest-to-God counterfeiter"

its chic to play the influence game but a great novels always at heart uninfluenced, for it has work to do of its own   *the recognitions* is very much its own book

names most often dropped: joyce by a mile* then wolfe & eliot   j & e

ulysses & *the recognitions* are very "20thcentury" & have a number of technical resemblances: both are long & closely organized; sharp contrast between humorous & nonhumorous passages; lots of blasphemy; modeling/parodies on classics & extensive crossreferences (*ulysses* having much more of former, *recognitions* of latter); "timegrowth" in rereading; many nonfictional references (miscalled "erudition") to give desired tones to the fiction; passion for other books; importance of ideas of major characters (dedalus, wyatt); delight in carry-ing humorous situations to extremes; restraint as basic technique of style   but the worlds of the 2 books arent alike, nor are the characters   the 2 have little resemblance in the essential   ie artistic   sense

42

are from the jacketback   alleged resemblance to wolfe a blackmark
for bloom bradley mccarthy because wolfe-gaddis, they dont resemble
nohow   except in cliche terms: wolfe wrote long novels, "ambitious"
novels & even (once) a 1st novel

names most often dropping: hartman managed 17, fremantle 8

playing the comparison game: gaddis inferior to other writers per 15
critics, equal—7, superior—1 (to *sironia, texas*)   purpose of the
game: to keep the new writers out

dashing off useless phrases on how a *character* reminds them of
one in another novel   invitation to critics to drive absurdity to its
limits:

His hero [Wyatt], a vague ineffectual wanderer, is rather like Kafka's
"K." (highet)

Mr. Pivner, the all-too-common man, is a try at redoing Joyce's Mr.
Bloom. (*time*)

bullshit!

& now, some sections on the cliches, those dearest possessions of the
critic   it takes work to see & write what a books own individual
qualities are   its easier to fall back on a cliche, to "work" from the
general to the particular   if you can read the number on the last
page of a novel, you can use—

the length cliche

—Reading it? Christ no, what do you think I am? I just been
having trouble sleeping, so my analyst told me to get a book and
count the letters, so I just went in and asked them for the thickest
book in the place and they sold me this damned thing, he muttered
looking at the book with intimate dislike. —I'm up to a hundred and
thirty-six thousand three hundred and something and I haven't even
made fifty pages yet. (*the recognitions* 936-7   the book the stubby
poet has is *the recognitions* itself)

a great *but* lengthy writer like Thomas Mann (berger   my italics)

a damaging confession!   the length cliches irrational—reading 1
long books no harder than reading 5 short ones   & its conformist—
not too long not too short, they wont attack you for a book of *average*
length

theres statistical evidence that readers of trashy superbestsellers
prefer a nice long one they can get their teeth into*   the critics
disagree because all that length, it hits them right in the hack!   they
dont get paid enough extra for long books & like the whores they are
they resent it

---

*john f harvey, *the content characteristics of best-selling novels* (unpublished
library sch phd dissertation, u of chicago 1949)

a novel over 300p can *have been* published (tolstoy, dostoyevsky, joyce) but it cant *now* be published—too much work for the critic. he has to hover over the same book too long, he might fall in

hear them whine, bellow, and scream:

inordinate length. (berger)

forbidding length (o'hearn)

almost interminable (morse)

interminable conversations (wagenknecht)

self-indulgent verbosity, deadly unfunny repetitiveness, and endless portentous gasping conversations (swados)

he could have, and should have, used the occasion to make some apology, however indirect, to all the reviewers who are forced to read his seemingly interminable tale. (hill)

a sort of monstrous annotation, a dropsical expansion of such scenes and moods as make up "The Waste Land." (rugoff)

AND SO WE dove in and floundered around through this literary Sargasso Sea until somehow we dragged ourselves on shore 956 pages later, completely pooped and the sole survivor. (bass)

When I complained recently to the people at the *Western Review* that I was tired of trying to consider half a dozen novels all at once, in a mass review, they must have decided to punish me. They asked if I would like to do a single novel, all by itself. I consented. Then they sent me *The Recognitions.* (hartman)

we are swollen and unrecognizable with the effort of trying to swallow so much. (fremantle)

at times an exasperating novel. This is not due alone to the tremendous volume of wordage (simak)

exasperating in its profligacy of diction (bloom)

maddeningly drawn out and unresolved (burnette)

To claim they give you 956 pages of novel in return for your money is like offering you a giant headache in return for your aspirin. (powell)*

the critics appeal to procrustes:

the physical labor of turning 900 pages when 300 would have been sufficient. (klein)

As a whole, the novel would profit considerably from a severe blue-penciling. (burnette)

not true   i have never read a novel that needed cutting—its a myth!

---

*this analogy requires careful thought, which it will not repay

an abridged *war and peace* is no improvement   i wish *the recognitions* was twice as long, because after 7 yrs ive used it up   itd be
worse if cut, perhaps crippled   thats what they want

> If Mr. Gaddis had wielded his shears with the same freedom that
> he wielded his pen, he might have produced a highly readable
> work. (dixon)

"wielded his shears" is offensive jargon, criticstyle   if the writer wont
cut, then let the parasites do it:

> It is a pity that, in his first novel, he did not have stronger editorial
> guidance than is apparent in the book—for he *can* write very well—
> even though most of the time he just lets his pen run on. (kirkus)

yes, the editors, the middlemen, the spoilers!   they cant create
themselves, itd be cruel to keep them from meddling with the creations of others:

> —But this book is about religion, said a sub-editor, standing aside
> for the tall man in the black Homburg to pass. —It's Buddhism.
> —But it's by a Jew, said the other, standing aside.
> —Well, I've told him if he'll change his hero from a Jew to a homo-
> sexual, we might accept it.
> —But that's the way it was in the first place.

(*the recognitions* 356-7)   no editor is competent to rewrite "his"
authors' books, much less unwrite them

> Gaddis writes with ease and vigor about a Greenwich Village
> gathering, but repeats this sequence many times. (kirkus)

5 short novels are better than 1 long one* but 1 long party scene is
better than 5 short ones   the unexamined contradiction shows cliche
thinking   same contradiction in bass & burnette—in burnette, not by
accident!

from frances burnette, *baltimore sun* 3/13/55	from virginia kirkus service 2/1/55
(1st sentence): "THE RECOGNITIONS" is another long and rather dreary saga of modern man in search of a soul, written around the theme of forgery—spiritual and emotional as well as material.	(1st phrase): This overlong (946 pages) and rather pretentious first novel concerns itself with the impasse of the modern intellectual
	(from the *recognitions* blurb): The pattern of forgery, emotional and spiritual as well as actual
Unfortunately, into its 956 pages the author has apparently tried to cram everything he knows, which is quite a lot, including mythology and ancient religious lore, painting, especially the early Flemish	He knows many odd facts about ancient religions—and he injects them all. He is familiar with many languages, and there are passages in Spanish, Italian, French,

*if prousts novel had been issued in 1 volume instead of 7, how the critics would
have howled!

school, music and languages. The book is generously sprinkled with Italian, French and Hungarian. The result is undisciplined and pretentious	German, Latin and even Hungarian. complete lack of discipline pretentious first novel
a broad canvas stretching from a small New England town to Rome, Paris, Madrid, a Central American outpost and New York city, particularly Greenwich Village where most of the action (that is, talk) takes place.	The scene is Spain, Rome and Paris in Europe, New York City (mainly Greenwich Village) and a New England town in the United States, and at moments an unnamed Central American Republic.
the son of a New England minister who gradually converts himself from Christianity to sun worship.	his father, a New England minister who converts himself to Mithraism—sun worship.
Although the book is highlighted by some brilliant writing, as in the biting description of a Greenwich Village cocktail party,* its effectiveness is dulled by too frequent repetition. Several such gatherings are described.	Gaddis writes with ease and vigor about a Greenwich Village gathering, but repeats this sequence many times.
(last sentence): As a whole, the novel would profit considerably from a severe blue-penciling.	(last sentence): It is a pity that, in his first novel, he did not have stronger editorial guidance than is apparent in the book—for he *can* write very well—even though most of the time he just lets his pen run on.

FIRE burnette for plagiarism

after paying his debt to editors the writer owes readers too   he should play back to them what they already think & are, ie write commercially

The average reader, who, Mr. Gaddis says, lacks intelligence, talent and sensitivity, will shun this appallingly enormous and enormously appalling catalog of intellectual and phony intellectual horrors, thereby disproving or proving Mr. Gaddis' statement. (laycock)

revanche!   critics   "ambitiously"   love to identify with the average reader, who like them cant create anything of value   & as the history of bestsellers shows prefers not to read anything of value

a catharsis for the writer rather than the reader. (rugoff)

Has an author the right to inflict this catharsis on us? The answer to that is in the enormity of the deed and the price. (laycock)

has he? ask aristotle   an author has the right to write as he god-

---

*there is no greenwich village cocktail party in *the recognitions* damn pleases   fuck the average reader!

(*the recognitions* never was overpriced $7.50—now $2.75—for a novel 5 times as long as average)

& the writer owes it to the reader to surrender his privacy:

> WILLIAM GADDIS, about whom his publishers are otherwise reticent, is 33 years old. (jackson)

> I do not feel that I know him from this book (hartman)

tough!   & one more debt   in *the recognitions* (243) valentine is speaking to wyatt about recktall brown:

> —Earlier, you know, he mentioned to me the idea of a novel factory, a sort of assembly line of writers, each one with his own especial little job. Mass production, he said, and tailored to the public taste. But not so absurd, Basil Valentine said sitting forward suddenly.
> —Yes, I . . . I know. I know.
> —When I laughed . . . but it's not so funny in his hands, you know. Just recently he started this business of submitting novels to a public opinion board, a cross-section of readers who give their opinions, and the author makes changes accordingly. Best sellers, of course.
> —Yes, good God, imagine if . . . submitting paintings to them, to a cross section? You'd better take out . . . This color . . . These lines, and . . .

critics whod shudder at such an idea, shudder with delight to think how some conceited genius will have to learn, after a few books flop, to write like they do:

> such readers as he may be fortunate enough to have (hicks)

> And if, please God, this book is not a "success," he may meet up with some human beings whom he can use as characters. Then perhaps he will really write. (hill)

the "ambitious" cliche

literally an ambitious writers one who must do the best work he can. hardly a criticism of him   but add innuendos & you have a powerful weapon against good books

(1) kennebeck speaks of "William Gaddis's frighteningly ambitious novel"   a revealing phrase!   "frightening"s intended to mean the reader wont have any fun   an "ambitious" novels sure to be long, difficult, dull, "what displeases"

> Ambitious, Challenging, Bulky (dawedeit headline)

> difficult, uncompromising, ambitious (highet)

> ambitious, difficult, bitter (hicks 5/23/59)

the reader must be ambitious too, he'll have to work too hard:

THE MOST AMBITIOUS novel in many seasons has arrived to challenge the judgment of ambitious readers. Not only its bulk but its density of style present obstacles to the unwary, and although style and content both contain ambiguities, one flat statement about the book can be made with confidence: Entertainment is not a primary objective. (dawedeit)

lazy reader dont buy!   but critics underrate readers   who arent *that* lazy after all   who read books voluntarily, not like critics doing work they hate for money

(2) implying the writer is only ambitious *personally:*

The author, who has spent seven years on it, evidently intends it to rival the most boldly original novels of the last generation. (highet)

ostentatiously aimed at writing a masterpiece (hicks)

as many critics have learned 1sthand, 7 yrs or 700 spent hoping to outdo other writers wont produce a novel at all, much less one like *the recognitions*   the critics cant even conceive a man may love his work   they defile art at the fountainhead

professor hartman uses the lively word trick   (a respectworthy book wouldnt "fling itself"):

For there is every indication that the author expects this work to fling itself directly into a class with, say, *Ulysses*—if not somewhat past that point.
There is, of course, nothing wrong with such an ambition. I am only sorry* to say that Mr. Gaddis does not quite make it, and I am all the sorrier because the amazing thing is that he does come close.

"of course"!   hartman manages to make a book which, he says, comes close to equaling or surpassing *ulysses,*** seem *by virtue of that fact* like a disgrace to its author   hes projecting his own unful-filled literary-*status* ambitions onto gaddis

(3) last & worst, "ambitious" can "prove" the writer failed   its the shoddy strawman trick: the writer is "ambitious"   hes trying to achieve a great deal   maybe more than he can do   why, hes reaching for the moon!   *it cant be that good*

ie as good as the *critic* said it might be   hicks & hartman lean heavily on this trick   even in a favorable review the cliche is auto-matic:

Very ambitious, it is powerful, if not always successful. (stocking)

all they ask is that the ambitious work have *nothing questionable* about it   at worst the a priori failure is "PROBLEMATICAL" & "pretentious" (kirkus)   at best its "in some respects an honest failure" (hayes) or "an honorable failure" (hicks 5/23/59)

---

*like a crocodile!

**to *balance* this hartmans next para begins: "Why then does the novel fail?" how can it do both

but "ambitious" novels are *not* usually failures   a guide for the lazy
but wellmeaning critic, how to recognize good books   exclude the
commercial trash, take the big "ambitious" novels & theyre usually the
good ones   dont read them just weigh them   once in a great
while such a books empty, phony like goodman's *the empire city.*
but most often its the good writer who takes the trouble to make a big
structure   the bad ones like to down tools early

i forgot, tho, the critics job is to make the good novels seem bad & the
bad ones good   he should say the good "ambitious" books fall short
of something   & the mediocre "pleasant" "modest" "appealing" books
succeed in something   & hope the reader wont see the 2 "somethings" are worlds apart

the 1st novel cliche

harvey swados disposes of this cliche in *the living novel* (171):

> I have myself done considerable reviewing of fiction, and can
> recall without difficulty a substantial group of first novels of the past
> few years which were in no way sentimental portraits of the artists
> as young men.

lists 1st novels by gold styron klein becker pawel malamud baldwin
gaddis & adds (172):

> in not one case do they correspond in intention or execution to the
> absurd conception of the American first novel as an adolescent
> portrait of adolescence.

all the less reason for swados   reviewing *the recognitions* in the
hudson review   to have postscripted a series of sarcastic blows
below the belt with the old 1st novel chestnut:

> I look forward with eager curiosity to see what he does next.

(however, theres also a 2d novel cliche by which all 2d novels are "dis-
appointing" & dont "live up to the promise" of the 1st)   price's
insight is better:

> it would be futile for the reviewer to rely upon a cliche and remark
> that "Gaddis, with his first novel, shows promise," for Gaddis has
> arrived, and he must be accepted—or rejected—for what he is and
> for what he says.

the critics can hardly say gaddis is a "young idealist" (with a headful of
foolish dreams) so hes a "young cynic" (he'll get over it):

Gaddis is a cynic but he's young. (desbarats)

Mr. Gaddis shows all the young cynic's naïveté (hill)

Soul-Searing
And Cynical (stevens headline*)

---

*other vulgarity prizes to headlinewriters for livingston, price, corrington:

the central attitude of *the recognitions* is not in fact cynical   still:

> For Mr. Gaddis (who, *by the way,* began this book eight years ago, when he was *about twenty-five years old*) sees ours as literally a society of forgeries, counterfeits, plagiarisms and fakes. (rugoff my italics)

he'll get over it!

all 1st novels are by definition autobiographical, therefore:

> The Recognitions is a non-literal novel, yet beneath its symbolism I detect a note of autobiography. The protagonist, Wyatt Gwyon, is a parson's son who has studied for the ministry and who has become by turns artist, commercial draftsman and forger of old master-pieces. I do not suggest that this is a literal account of Mr. Gaddis' career, or that he has in his family tree anyone like the Rev. Gwyon, who went mad and sacrificed a bull on Christmas Day and tried to introduce his staid New England congregation to Mithra-worship. A similarity of background, however, would explain the author's pre-occupations. (o'hearn)

which implies   however cagily   that wyatt is gaddis   otherwise, since in a sense of course every character comes out of its author, the para need not have been written   even more stupid guess:

> the character Otto, a self-conscious young playwright for whom Gaddis himself may have posed (dawedeit)

the vanity of time and *the recognitions* by the same person!   why not guess stanley, anselm, valentine, recktall brown?   the joke on the autobiographical clicheteers is that gaddis *does* appear in *the recognitions*—as "willie," a comic minor character   whose role, naturally, is to get off alltoowellprepared witticisms only to find no one is listening:

> —Philogyny? I thought you said phylogeny.
> —I said, misogyny recapitulates philogyny.
> —Misogamy . . . ?
> —Never mind.
> —What's the name of this book you're writing?
> —Baedeker's *Babel.*
> Noting only the striped tie on the taller of these two, Otto brought the handkerchief up again, and got by them.
> —And you say you've become a misologist?

(p475   takeoff on haeckel's "ontogeny recapitulates phylogeny." misogyny: hatred of women   philogyny: love of women   misogamy: hatred of marriage   misology: hatred of rational discussion or philosophy)   "Baedeker's *Babel*" is *the recognitions* (see p372-3, 936-7)   when last seen willie is working for a tv studio:

Hefty Novel Hits Negative Note

First Novel Sure to Stir Up Storm;
Assails All Phases of Civilization

Mammoth Novel by William Gaddis Bemoans
Modern Man's Insatiable Lust for Fakery

50

The long bare corridor was brightly lighted and empty, until a young man with a thin face, a slightly crooked nose, and a weary expression which embraced his whole appearance, passed them. —There, there's the guy who was working on this, he's one of the writers. Hey, Willie . . . But the weary figure went on. He was carrying two books, one titled, *The Destruction of the Philosophers,* the other, *The Destruction of the Destruction.* He rounded a corner away from them muttering, —Christ. Christ, Christ, Christ, Christ, Christ.

(p734   an example of "timegrowth" & postreading shock of recognition, when i read this passage i assumed the 2 booktitles were humorous inventions   this year, proofreading a not too fascinating bibliography of medieval philosophy, the 2 titles jumped to my eyes. the 1st is by algazel, an arab moslem c 1100 ad   it attempts to refute doctrines of philosophers (aristotle & avicenna) opposed to koran   the 2d is by averroes, to refute the 1st   so after 7 yrs willie as negativist (or "positive negativist") becomes also misologist andor philologist)

when a "long" novels also a "1st" novel the critics must leap to—

the "undisciplined" cliche

who wrote these gems?

He may have a theme. The material may even be connected in his own mind. If so, the connections are not made clear to me. Such lack of selectivity as is here manifested I have never encountered in a novel before; Thomas Wolfe was a mosaic worker in comparison.

He is the only individual that the writer has encountered outside of a madhouse who has let flow from his pen random and purposeful thoughts just as they are produced. He does not seek to give them orderliness, sequence or interdependence.

1st is edward wagenknecht reviewing *the recognitions* without bothering to finish it

2d is dr joseph collins in the *ny times*   its his 5/28/22 review of joyces *ulysses*   the worldrecord review for avoiding onesidedness by "balancing" statements far too pro & con to be reconciled:

pro:	con:
"Ulysses" is the most important contribution that has been made to fictional literature in the twentieth century. It will immortalize its author.	The average intelligent reader will glean little or nothing from it— even from careful perusal, one might properly say study, of it— save bewilderment and a sense of disgust.
Mr. Joyce had the good fortune to be born with a quality which the world calls genius.	It requires real endurance to finish "Ulysses."
	I am probably the only person, aside from the author, that has ever read it twice from beginning to end.

& adds: "I have learned more psychology and psychiatry from it than I did in ten years at the Neurological Institute"   its neuropathological to write that *ulysses* has no "orderliness, sequence or interdependence"   & just as mad to make the same criticism of *the recognitions*

the legitimate question would be if the 2 books are *over*disciplined, *ulysses* by its analogies to homer & vico, *the recognitions* by its intricate network of crossreferences   bachs music gives many a proof that art can easily carry a formal burden (eg canons) that   to the inquiring *mind*   seems obviously insupportable   in writing too, the lively existence of joyces great novel answers the theoretical question   & in *the recognitions* the complex framework of reference & crossreference doesnt interfere at all with the life, vividness of the characters & events, but magnifies them, gives them added colors & "timegrowth"

i open *the recognitions* at random   its p593, well into esther's darwinian party   the "scent of lavender" has a long history in the book, eg used for forgery by both wyatt & sinisterra   when its esthers sister rose who mentions the poem "A magnet hung in a hardware shop" it takes on mysterious connotations   irony, actually its a silly song from gilbert & sullivan   the music (too loud), voices (like waves), benny (moving to desperation), esthers kitten (moving thru various themes of mistreatment to its death), the little girl from downstairs (collecting sleeping pills a few at a time for her mothers suicide)   are all brought back over & over, in separated snatches at the party till their development is done   making new echoes at each rereading   lines 17-21 ("cigarette somewhere"—see p639 line 30) & 23-25 ("*he*" is the *trees of home* author, not wyatt) are 2 of many episodes in the book where someone says whats exactly in key with feelings youre hiding, you answer & it turns out thats not what was meant   "best sellers" has a number of crossreferences & "My husband says he stole the plot from the Flying Dutchman, whoever that is" is one of dozens of such items of "forged culture"—& the dutchman, in or out of wagners opera, appears on other pp   "Some faggot writes them for me"—see p314 line 23 for the crossreference. & so it goes, not a phrase without a definite purpose or purposes

no one who knows *the recognitions* at all would say its undisciplined. thats like saying dostoyevskys characters "lack intensity" or strindbergs *a dream play* is "sordid realism"   14 of 55 reviewers *did* say it! for just one cliche reason: a "long 1st novel" must *by definition* be "undisciplined" & "sprawling":

But the main fault of the novel is a complete lack of discipline. (kirkus)

judgment and discipline, but these are qualities which he plainly lacks. (hill)

"chaos novel" (powell)

It is a sprawled giant of a book, with little plot but a great deal to say. (demarest)

The book has the formless disjointed quality of a nightmare. (parke)

to date the one valid criticism of Wolfe is his lack of discipline. In comparison with Gaddis, Wolfe wore a literary strait-jacket. (simak)

formlessness . . . an uncontrolled exhibition* . . . Like a poem it coheres only in spirit (rugoff   my ellipses)

& bradley ("sprawling" "undisciplined and baffling prose"), burnette ("undisciplined and pretentious" "sprawling prose"), klein ("sprawling"), mcalister ("the writing is undisciplined"), o'hearn ("undisciplined and unfulfilled"), stocking ("vast, sprawling")**

the cliche is so tempting that when mccarthy wrote:

tightly knit despite seeming nebluousness [sic]

his headlineman, skimming thru the review as careless as the critics skimmed thru *the recognitions,* read it the way it *should* be:

Brilliant Flashes Illumine
Sprawling, Inchoate Novel

this cliche about *this* book is such a dead giveaway of not having really read it that their bosses must FIRE bradley demarest mcalister o'hearn parke rugoff simak & stocking, to mention only those not already axed

the erudition cliche

in *the recognitions* are hidden booktitles & quotes from shakespeare. many facts about early catholic church alchemy mythology   many nonfictional references they add a lot to the novel as a novel:

---

*not "superbly disciplined" like *the waste land*

**of course the prose in *the recognitions* is no less disciplined than the form

are critics disciplined?   eg, of 38 quotes of ten words or more from *the recognitions* they misquoted 25   of 21 critics making such quotes 18 got at least one wrong   (original reviews only)

most misquotes were careless but involved at most meddling with commas & capitals   but give an american lesion prize to livingston for censoring out the terrible words "damn it" & "Chrahst"   & coldwell for changing "unchristian" to "un-Christian"

a misrepresentation prize to boss smith for making gaddis an ungrammarian:

the recognitions, p946	as quoted by smith (my italics)
Any city that calls herself modern anticipates all her children's needs, even to erecting something high for them to jump from	Any city which calls *itself* modern anticipates all *her* children's needs, even to erecting something high for them to jump from

a quotesmanship award to the *new yorker* hack for quoting p50 lines 9-15 out of context & without explaining the crossreferences, thus fraudulently giving the impression that all of *the recognitions* is esoteric, incomprehensible & just "words, words, words"   & to bass who quotes a 5-line list of books from p23 & says "lists like the following for page after page after page after page"   its a lie, no such list is more than a few lines long

(1) for "timegrowth"   changing of the book as its reread & new references are recognized (see p50 above)

(2) defining the book's "world"   eg the harlem drag party gets another dimension, more reality from the history material (*the recognitions* 311-2 315-6)   eg parallel of faust-poodle-mephistopheles to wyatt-black poodle-recktall brown extends the meaning of forgery in the novel (135 136-40)

(3) the characterization gets richer   eg the assault on *how to win friends & influence people* (497-503) is itself good nonfiction   but in *the recognitions* its functions to show mr pivner from another angle. his actions are so weak & restricted that hed seem unreal, thinly characterized without some such background to interact with

not one of the critics saw it   that gaddis book isnt a novel *plus*   for no good reason   lectures on flemish painting etc, but a novel that uses nonfiction for fictional purposes   critics think nonfictions for its own sake, result: the erudition cliche

"awesome erudition"   astonishing astounding awe-inspiring fearsome immense monstruous phenomenal prodigious tremendous unmatched & vast!*   why does gaddis "learning" "scholarship" "knowledge" drive the critics adjectivemad   extended "erudition" for fictional tones is rare, gaddis being different & must be penned in the wildanimal cage, fiercely labeled

some critics tho, dont concede him any "astounding" erudition:

    half-digested learning. (north)

    What erudition the book contains—and it lays claim to much— seems to be largely reducible to the *Golden Bough* and a college course in comparative religion. (hill)

wrong complaint, a source bibliography of facts that are painted into *the recognitions* would be very long   the "erudition"'s extensive, usually not intensive but anecdotal, odds & ends picked up from everywhere   *encyclopaedia britannica* or a primary source, it doesnt matter   a novels not a phd thesis

    He works in a good deal of esoteric learning (quotations in Latin and other weird languages,** recondite historical allusions), although unfortunately not without mistakes here and there. (highet)

doesnt matter either   nonfiction references in *ulysses* arent "without mistakes" & whats so unfortunate about that? theres been no rush to trade *ulysses* in for a sound book of mathematical tables***

rugoff says adding "ideas of the church fathers" "quotations, echoes

---

*key #s 15   36 67 13 36 21&39&52 16 62 41 40 69 59&67

**joke—highet latin professor at columbia

****recognitions* errata list conflicts with unusual value in novel (not necessarily to be taken as advice to reader) that its good if characters speak several languages faultlessly, quote exactly from anything theyve read & have no intellectual accidents   but its a minor conflict

and parodies" results in a mixture not a fusion   but just as in
ulysses, adding references & crossreferences may be a mixture technique but the results a fusion   because (1) characters are there,
genuinely created, for the nonfiction to fuse with   (2) the "erudition"s tied in specifically & flexibly, not like the mixture in *war & peace.*
fusion: when the wholes more than the sum of its parts

critics dont know what that book larnins doing in a novel so they
mostly disapprove:

> an encyclopedia is not a work of art. (berger)

> Unfortunately, into its 956 pages the author has apparently tried to
> cram everything he knows (burnette)

> the polysyllables, sentence fragments and foreign words give the
> novel too "arty" a tone. (dixon)

works arty when formal devices are substituted for content the artist
cant supply   *the recognitions* isnt that kind of impoverished work.
dixon means highbrow or egghead not "arty"

> one is forced to reflect that erudition is not necessarily wisdom.
> (price)

& *therefore . . .*

or unnecessary erudition, overused:

> excessive deployment of the author's phenomenal erudition (rolo)

> too frequently obscured by unnecessary erudition. (mcalister)

> repetitious parade of erudition (laycock)

or angrier (comparing *recognitions* riches with their own little bag of
cliches & stale tags):

> Somebody arrives in Paris, and we get the whole background of
> Paris history before we go on with it. (wagenknecht)

> Wyatt Gwyon and Wyatt's creator, whose combined erudition is as
> annoying as Philo Vance's (o'hearn)

> a hail of erudition poured like boiling oil on the defenseless heads
> not of his enemies but of his readers (or does he intend an
> identity?).
>   It is precisely this last question which makes us uneasy: is it just
> the *others* whom he is assaulting, or is he after *us* too? (swados)

just the others!

> The reader scampering to catch the ever-defaulting hero in his
> many guises through bordellos and monasteries is exasperated by
> Author Gaddis, as Ancient Mariner, waylaying him with lectures on
> the Church Fathers, the Antichrist, Descartes or the "Book of the
> Dead." (powell)

& then on to projecting their own sweet selves   gaddis must be putting in that descartes stuff *just to show off:*

> a writer of showy if spotty erudition and a determination to exploit it
> (o'hearn)

> a wealth of religious reference which, meaningful as it may be to
> the expert, too often seems like so much theological name drop-
> ping. (*newsweek*)

> [A list of books] may let you know that old Gaddis is a whiz with the
> reference cards in the library, but it adds very little to the novel in
> information about characters or insight into events. (bass)

> suggests forcibly the man who just can't bear not to have you, the
> reader, know every minute how tremendously knowledgeable he is.
> (jackson)

fullestscale attack on "erudition" was of course in a highbrow quarterly, the *hudson review*   harvey swados remarks on fun made of
"The phoney editor of a phoney literary magazine" & tourists "butcher-
ing Spanish and murdering French":

> as we press on through Mr. Gaddis's heavy artillery fire (I counted
> eight different languages *en route,* and there may well have been
> *more*) we begin to suspect that his contempt may extend to all
> those who know less than he.

(how much less?)   it isnt that otto doesnt know spanish well that
makes the satire, but that he thinks knowing a few words is good
enough because its *he* who knows them (vanity)   swados continues:

> It is necessarily intensified when we meet the phoney distinguished
> novelist holed up in a Spanish monastery, gathering material for a
> quickie on religion and the simple life, with his "book of quotations,
> which stood him in the stead of a classical education". This kind of
> fun verges on the mean (who nowadays *does* have a classical
> education?) and exposes the book's biggest weakness.

this time its not vanity but forgery   implied satirical point isnt that
ludy hasnt a classical education but that he *pretends* to have one by
sticking in greek-latin items from the book of quotations   swados
doesnt know the real function of "erudition" in a novel so he thinks its
the same as in the *hudson review:*

> biggest weakness.
>   Mr. Gaddis has fallen victim to his own erudition. Unable to resist
> the temptation to prove that he is as familiar with ecclesiastical
> history as a professor at a theological seminary, as at home in
> many languages, including the Hungarian, as the dean of a Berlitz
> School,* as conversant with graphic art as a museum director, he
> has strangely forgotten** that erudition isn't even necessary for the
> creation of good and true fiction

---

*swados has the naive idea that gaddis "has apparently made an enormous
effort to assimilate" "all of western culture"   but at the moment youre still
allowed to write novels without the full professorship   actually the hungarian
phrases in *the recognitions* were picked up by asking a few questions in the bar
of a hungarian restaurant

**crooked!

56

what a criterion!   murders not necessary for good & true fiction,
therefore *the brothers karamazov* shouldnt have included one

& heres to 1 reviewer feeling no pain:

> The constant use of literary allusions and book titles in the narra-
> tive fascinated this librarian. (herbert cahoon, curator of autograph
> mss & later printed books, morgan library)

the "difficult" cliche

a rich novels always "difficult"   unless you hug impoverishment why
worry?

the recognitions is a pleasure to reread—& also to read the 1st time,
but not if you treat it like a textbook each paragraph of which has to
be mastered before going on to the next:

> Most readers will find it difficult, if not impossible, to read the full
> 956 pages of this novel with the careful attention Mr. Gaddis would
> like. (mcalister)

> The reader may find the going rough and uncertain, but keeps plod-
> ding along. (yeiser)

here the plodding readers the *serious* reader, the *partisan review*
reader, the textbook grind   but its lively curiosity   not careful
strained attention or "intense scholarly analysis"* (*newsweek*)   that
will lead you to dig for more treasure, if not on 1st reading then later.
in the meantime, no need to panic because somethings not clear.
read on! lifting each foot well off the ground

the critics   "rejecting the shell without looking for the pearl"**   en-
vision the tooserious reader but they have the opposite flaw   their
ideals to race thru once carelessly, taking fast notes & faking a review
without ever having made contact with the book   have you ever
read a novel much too fast?   the scenes skim by like a spedup
movie & you get a weird sensation of total contactlessness, of not
knowing the characters in the book, not knowing anything, not knowing yourself   simak reports this exact experience:

> a puzzling, and at times an exasperating novel. This is not due
> alone to the tremendous volume of wordage, but to a willful, de-
> liberate abstruseness on the part of the author. At no time does he
> level with the reader; he conducts an intricate game of hare-and-
> hound in which a panting reader strives desperately to catch up
> with him and at times tries futilely to understand what actually has
> happened. This gives to the whole work a certain vicious dream-like
> character—the kind from which you wake up, if not screaming, at
> least badly befuddled.

---

*"A FEW intuitive, sensitive visionaries may understand and comprehend
'Ulysses,' James Joyce's new and mammoth volume, without going through a
course of training or instruction, but the average intelligent reader . . ." (dr joseph
collins, *ny times* 5/28/22)

**henri peyre, *writers and their critics* (ithaca ny 1944) 218

by definition a "difficult" novels unclear obscure & vague:

"The Recognitions" is difficult, obscure and confusing. I have grave doubts about the permanent value of books that put obstacles in the way of the reader's understanding. (parke)

His dialogue is often too cryptic to follow and his introductions of new characters to a situation and even his introductions of new situations are frequently so vague that the reader is forced to reread several paragraphs and sometimes pages. (mcalister)

He maintains no single story line, he seldom introduces or directly identifies his characters, he switches from one to another with only a hint of explanation, he describes vital episodes from odd angles so that they cannot be grasped at first reading (highet)

tragic—for the speeding critic

the compassion cliche

the slogan of the sonofabitch, the philistine, the enemy of art   "compassion"!   1 of those cult words, swollen, a monster

like "communication"   this word has a real meaning, refers to a minor technical problem in writing   if the reader has to go to the same laundry as the writer to know what hes talking about, the writer has failed to communicate   or if the writer has the irritating "beat" habit of putting his friends names in poems so they can see themselves in print   easy to avoid, anyway an occasional lapse in this kind of "communication" doesnt matter*   but as overblown lately "communication"s the catchword of those who go sleepless because not all writers will join them in the literary whorehouse   it means, write mush   (chief ingredient: instant understanding)   like in the *reader's digest*

or   with due regard for p395-6, 951-2 of *the recognitions*   "maturity"   it just means growing up   i admit most of us dont do that but   "maturity" as a cult word means a *fake* growingup—really a burningout   psychopaths reform in jail at 60, they burn out & dont have to be criminals or anything else   & you too, when youve had enough vitality beaten out of you   can stop "behaving like a spoiled child" without ever having grown up   a result much prized by advice-columnists & constructors of the fake novel

"compassion"s empathy   a natural sense often replaced by something more radioactive lately   but the overblown "compassion"—remember the old novels, last chapter the zero & zeroine "marry & live happily ever after"   if only another chapter would try & show how they manage it!   (their sexual incapacity   "chastity"   having been spelled out at booklength)   in the 20thcentury version   sophisticated   of fake happyending the hero burns out to "maturity"   hes attained "compassion" *by learning to project his selfpity onto others*

---

*no, *the recognitions* is not "strictly personal, often incomprehensible to others" (desbarats, whose reviews so vague & general i wonder if he read the book)

58

the commercial writer turns his selfpity into "compassion"   the
reader just rewinds, 1st he "identifies with the characters"   then he
wallows in selfpity   the trouble with the trick   as with all critics
ideals & "crucial ingredients"   is that its too easy & unrewarding.
anyone *can* write with heartrendering compassion (see the confession-
mags) as anyone can write commercial hardcore pornography or
describe a steak so your mouth waters   good writers wont do un-
skilled labor they dont live up to the critics ideal & can be compared
unfavorably to bad writers which is what the critic had in mind all
along   like the "ambitious" cliche the compassion cliches a strong
weapon against great art

a 20thcentury novel, *the recognitions* isnt emotionally demonstrative,
wears no heart on sleeve   it does have a subtle, touching empathy
for love, the unspoken hopeless loves of esme or recktall brown for
wyatt, hannah for stanley, inononu for valentine   it has none of the
sickening compassion/sympathy of the clichemongers:

> It is immensely long and immensely erudite, and for the first few
> hundred pages continuously disturbing, rather than interesting.*
> (*new yorker*)

whats disturbings always interesting   but oh for a nice little novel
about nice little people!—

> One reads on, hoping to have one's sympathies engaged, but they
> never are; little by little, it turns out that disturbingness is all. Mr.
> Gaddis appears to know every last thing about his characters
> except how to make them touch our hearts. To conceal the lack of
> this crucial ingredient of any novel, or perhaps to show his con-
> tempt for it, he dazzles us with words, words, words (*new yorker*)

drop the cold heartless *recognitions* & try a typical sympathyengaging
new yorker story   the plot: an executive is young, happilymarried
with 2 cleareyed kids, semiaristocratically handsome, kempt, makes
$14000 a year   1 morning on his way to the office *something fright-
fully embarrassing happens to him*

célines proof having "one's sympathies engaged" (cf geismar) is no
crucial ingredient   cant phrases like this & "touch our hearts" touch
rather my vomiting center   whether used to damn, or to praise in
high criticstyle:

> A novel of many and obvious flaws, always difficult of meaning,
> often confused in structure and style, it yet plagues the mind,
> impresses the memory, and touches the heart. (hayes)

price like the *new yorker* ties uncompassion to gaddis "contempt":

> If the author has anything above utter contempt for mankind, I
> have failed to detect it; if he has a sense of compassion, he has
> succeeded in concealing it.

> His wit, everywhere apparent, somehow has little pleasantry; rather
> it is often of a texture so hard and merciless as to resemble a
> curious sort of cruelty.

---

*the same whopping judgment boner geismar made

my guess is he thinks the caricatured characters are all the characters
& that the caricature sections, with their blistering judgments usual
to satire, are a sociology treatise on "what people are really like."
would he make the same judgment of molière?

The author, whose creations these characters are, has no more
sypmathy [sic] for them than they have for each other, so by the
end of the book he contrives to have them killed off one by one,
some more or less credibly. For others he conveniently arranges
cataclysms, which have no artistic validity because their fate has
been made to seem of no importance. Take the attitude of Mrs.
Deigh, the foolish rich American type, theatrically religious, who
lives in Rome and who has installed stained-glass windows in her
Daimler. She says to Stanley, "The newspaper never tells us nice
things. Sometimes it just pipes in more blood than we think we can
endure. And when you mentioned our daughter, didn't you. We
knew there was something, and now we remember. I was sure I'd
read in the newspaper that she's been hung for murder. Murdering
her husband! And that is a little too much to endure, even for one's
own flesh and blood."* (yeiser)

its not her daughter but another woman with a similar name (p294
915)   mrs deigh does think its her daughter but theres no law
gaddis has to make mrs deigh give a shit about her daughters death.
if she doesnt thats no fault of *the recognitions*

the many deaths toward the end of the book   at this point i should
retire for a pinchhitter who thinks shakespeare did more than write a
few perfect lines when he felt like it—every few years   the pinchhitter could set up a defense behind the deathlists in *king lear* &
*hamlet***

many coincidences in *the recognitions*   if a character walks a block
hes sure to run into 3 others   sometimes coincidence for comedy
(otto meeting sinisterra)   sometimes for the books closeknitness,
gives another inevitability to its "world" by tying the characters up
close to the exclusion of the actual world   the coincidences work
well: the literally unbelievable makes the books world more believable,
more there

i think the multiple deaths have somewhat the same justification as
the coincidences (& express the thematic "no" of the last part)   *the
recognitions* usually presents death as comic, without empathy   the
deaths work on the pp where they happen but personally i dont think
they work well in relation to the book as a whole***   for this yeiser
gives exactly the wrong reason: the comic deaths *would* work if the
characters' fate had "been made to seem of no importance" & if they
dont work its because the characters' fate has taken on *too much*
importance (esther, sinisterra, stanley)

yeisers "sympathy for" the characters is the usual 1-dimensional
cliche   why always sympathy, why not love, hate, fear, laugh at
them   or be judged by them (wyatt & esme)   why only *one*

the recognitions 914-5   misquoted

**of main characters: 7 in 10, 6 in 7

***& in general the last part is just noticeably weaker, less lit

response & such a tepid stereotype*   do lovers look at each other
with "compassion"?   should you feel "sympathy" for myshkin?
what presumption!

per hartman, gaddis fails because hes not like joyce who "remains
always human or compassionate, even when he is enraged"   but per
o'hearn, g fails because he "lacks the malignant spark which sustained
the Irishman"   & per corrington, g succeeds because he simply drips
with compassion:

> has managed from the beginning to underscore the tragedy of his
> time with an immense compassion for the pathetic human beings
> who are smashed in the complex machinery of their own devising.
>   It is a controlled and mature compassion but it lends to "The
> Recognitions" the tone of humanity that must be present if a work
> is to be truly great.

an unfortunate concession to a false standard

the "negative" cliche

the compassion cliches twin   rare the great writer not met with complaints about gloomspreading, bitter negative attitude   refusal to
forge silverlinings   length of this section shows "negative"s the
favorite cliche of the hacks   who're amazed   at each good new
novelist because the poor bastards so dumb he cant even learn to nod
his head instead of shaking it

its easy to fake a positive attitude but creations something else   a
few *recognitions* critics spurn the cliche:

> To demonstrate a thesis which is in its concrete form pessimistic
> but in its ultimate desire optimistic, Gaddis fires at us—repeatedly
> and contrapuntally, exquisitely and vulgarly—various manifestations
> of man's self-deception. (bloom)

> Gaddis is a cynic but he's young. Cynicism 100 per cent can't
> write a book. Gaddis smashes hypocrisy with a real hate but when-
> ever he lays something in ruins he discovers. Reading his book
> makes one look at the world through dark-colored glasses that filter
> out all but the strong, true light. Only reflections are lost. (desbarats)

> The fault with the novel, if such there is, rests not with the writer
> but with the all-too-realistic characters that people his pages—and
> with a society that has spawned a whole galaxy of forgery and
> accepted it as real.
>   Gaddis might be termed guilty of an unforgivable crime: He has
> seen too much and has recreated it too well. He has produced a
> range of characterization that blankets the deceit and cowardice of
> our generation. (corrington)

but theyre way outnumbered   a few negation negaters:

> There is a bite, a dig, a little bit of sickness in everything that
> happens and after a while you begin to hope that some day Gaddis

---

*"compassion" means *no* passion

might meet a nice girl and settle down in a vine-covered cottage with a white picket fence because he's had it and the change might do him good. (bass)

Of all the recent maledictions pronounced upon modern man, the almost interminable invective of "The Recognitions" is certain to achieve some special sort of notoriety. (morse)

Unfortunately "The Recognitions" does not persuade us that it is based on any but a narrow and jaundiced view, a projection in part of private discontent. It is a clinical collection of slides showing organisms of decay magnified grotesquely and stained to an unnatural vividness. (rugoff)

"The Recognitions" is undoubtedly the most nihilistic piece of important writing since Ernest Hemingway's "A Clean, Well Lighted Place." (mccarthy)

(*the recognitions* is undoubtedly not nihilistic at all)

Gaddis' nightmare world, a world which, though there is no person in it you would like to meet, nevertheless exercises a fascination over the reader. (parke)

I deplore the spirit of an age in which joy of life is completely lacking. Tragedy, horror, pettiness all have a place in art but in the long run the great books have affirmed life, not denied it. But it is possible that my vision is short, that these drab, petty, despairing people who really do not find life worth living, express the spirit of our age and will still live and speak to another generation. (parke)

great books dont affirm or deny "life"   its there, isnt it? cheeryouup books dont affirm anything, dont stimulate   they only depress the depression   *the recognitions* is one of the few books that have changed my life thru expression of positive values   it didnt give me a campaignbutton inscribed "i like people"   but it showed, without romanticizing, what life can be like without vanity (wyatt, esme)

(1) novelist & reporter arent the same job   itd be no flaw if *the recognitions* presented the world worse than it is   (2) it doesnt

negative cliche: hartman

"negative"s the main cliche prof carl hartman used in the *western review*   FIRE him—or me if his parody of quarterly criticism was on purpose

his 5p padded review starts with a complaint about the length of *the recognitions*   he signals a talent for projection & refusal to let imagination be confined by reality:

And we are not allowed to overlook this otherwise mundane matter of length, for the book seems almost passionately to assert some obscure tenet which holds that concentrated prolificness ought somehow to be associated with profundity and quality, and the implication would appear to be that there is a cause-and-effect relationship.

the implications all hartmans, part of his struggle with his conscience (he wins) which tells him he knows the book *is* of the highest quality & he has no business attacking it   the book is intense, wordy, bitter, experimental, obscure as to place, carefully confused as to person, he says

> And all of this is in a subtle way involved in the very *fact* of the book's length, its special kind of bulk.

he doesnt name the "subtle way" for the good reason that it doesnt exist   then the "ambitious" smear:

> there is every indication that the author expects this work to fling itself directly into a class with, say, *Ulysses*—if not somewhat past that point.

gaddis is "skillful, talented, prolific, inexhaustible, brilliant" etc. "Why then does the novel fail?"

> I am going to go out on a limb and say that the failure is very simple in nature: it is a failure of heart, a lack of what used to be called "love".

most best 20thcentury writing (including joyce) lacks it   if you require every work of art to have every quality you can attack them all. the courageous "I am going to go out on a limb" starts a chain of buffooneries:

> Let me say at once that I do not presume to condemn Mr. Gaddis simply on the grounds of his negations, or merely because his style seems to convey a sense of *eternal and deep-rooted hatred for the human race.* I would in fact join with him in *a vast displeasure with Society.* I too am *fond* of Herbert Marshall McLuhan's *The Mechanical Bride,* and I am *fondest* of Huxley when he is being most bitter.

(my italics except for booktitle)   he satirizes the insidedope school of academic criticism:

> I will go along with a good deal of "G. Legman's" *Love and Death*

("G. Legman"s real name is G. Legman)   he objects not to malcolm lowry, mailer, dreiser, arthur miller—except the last 2 *arent negative enough*   (this leaves him no room to attack *the recognitions* as "too negative"   hes going to attack it as "entirely negative")   suddenly hes writing about a stocking ad he saw in *life* magazine   he lingers over it for a whole page   (gaddis in spite of his "just plain wordiness" would have managed in a sentence)   both he & gaddis would "feel scorn" for *life* ads & drivein churches but

> I think that what Mr. Gaddis has forgotten is that before Joyce wrote *Finnegan's Wake** he wrote *Ulysses,* and before *Ulysses* he wrote *Portrait,* and before *Portrait* he wrote *Dubliners.* This is important not because the "simpler" stories of *Dubliners* help us straighten out mechanical details in *Finnegan's Wake,** but because such stories as "Clay" or "The Dead" are first of all Joyce's essential

---

*sic, professor!

affirmation of his philosophical-emotional stand toward this universe, the positive kind of stand which must underlie any meaningful negations

a truism not worth using   & gaddis novel *does* have this underlayer

and which we must be aware of if we are going to be able to place the later Joyce in any really intelligible philosophical frame of reference.

& on the reference shelf of the college library   hartmans implications false, all joyces work   the savagely bitter "clay"   "the dead," essentially not affirmative but regretful (cf *the recognitions* 14)   & even *finnegans wake*   is about as "negative" as gaddis work

Whether it is because of the existence of these early stories that Joyce remains always human or compassionate, even when he is enraged, is a question I cannot answer; but it is beside the point, which is that Joyce *does* always remain so. And I think that the same is true of Flaubert, of Huxley, of Dreiser, of Swift, or anybody who has vented his fury upon mankind in such a way that mankind is not forced to lose its basic respect for the writer.

as you lose respect in a mutualadmiration society (ltd) when the contract is broken   those named are as "negative" as gaddis—swift more

I am aware that I am in danger of sounding like early reviews of the works of all of the above, especially Joyce.

im aware a possibility can be admitted & still be true   hartman would have attacked *ulysses* at 1st publication, it would have upset him much the same as *the recognitions* does

I must hold, however, that we are not talking here about "obscenity" or some other absurd social viewpoint; and we have the great advantage of hindsight, which we may use to look at this present work.

& make false comparisons to it (see céline below)

we have no right to transmute phenomena of the past into rules for the present, and it could possibly be argued that Mr. Gaddis has simply transcended the stupid old humanitarian limitations of the past and thus produced a work which is deliberately and triumphantly entirely negative in its philosophical outlook;

so he sneaks in his Big Lie   *of course* the books not "entirely negative" what about gwyon wyatt esme stanley what about section i what about every page   but the strawmans set up:

and it could be argued further that this is only right and proper. We have to admit that in theory this argument has to be ruled valid: we must never be given the right to tell an author what he can and cannot say.

especially when he didnt say it   strawman attacked:

64

if Mr. Gaddis' only indication that people are worth looking at as *people* is his tremendous expenditure of energy to tell them that they are not, what can the book really have to say to us? Even Céline, with all his destructive force, does not approach Mr. Gaddis' insatiable desire for a statement of absolute and complete negation.* I do not for a moment question the morality of Mr. Gaddis' view, but I am forced to question the wisdom of perfectly unqualified condemnation: Is its philosophical level any higher than that of perfectly unqualified praise?

strawman demolished**   now hartman descends from philosophic clouds for an amazing spite session:

A small example: Mr. Gaddis does not like doctors, or the medical profession in general, and he takes great delight in telling us about how these fellows go about keeping alive people who would be better off dead, or otherwise mistreating mankind. I do not quarrel with this thesis, up to a certain point, and my favorite passages in Proust are those in which we are told various means of confusing addleheaded physicians. But then Mr. Gaddis gets hold of a character who suffers from diabetes, and who must therefore give himself insulin shots. I admit from the start that there is something absurd about the procedure of giving oneself shots of anything at all; but does this furnish sufficient reason to embark on a tirade against all of Science, which has foolishly provided this obstacle to a disease? Or, does it provide a genuine cause for us to despise this particular man? Would Mr. Gaddis really prefer that the character we are speaking of just go into a state of shock, so as to avoid any compromise with Society, or Science? And if the character *did* act that way, would Mr. Gaddis then consider him heroic? But that would appear to be impossible, to judge from the tone of the book, for Mr. Gaddis first of all would never permit a hero. You can see what a philosophical tangle we have gotten into already, without half trying. [!] But one further question: Would Mr. Gaddis himself really suffer the state of shock rather than surrender? If so, I say more power to him, though I am given no cause to think that he would.

(i swear im not making this up!)

However, the important thing here is the fact that the real ambiguity of his position—whatever it is—has not been fully stated.

there seems to be some confusion here   hartman has it wrong that *the recognitions* is a "polemic" & not "a true novel"   the double value   to be sure, not "fully stated" as in a polemic   is a main nonrealistic value (it works very well) in the book   its that some

---

*obviously célines more "negative" than gaddis   the central attitude in célines 2 best novels is (1) all eloquence idealism love & the "positive" are selfserving lies (2) people are disgusting   (& a more honest attitude than say faulkners silly nobelprize speech)

**not quite!   every condemnation does imply a positive value & this makes it seem an "entirely negative" novel cant be written   but go from algebra-logic to calculus   imagine a novel whose each positive value is exposed as false & hypocritical, producing another implied positive value in turn exposed as false & ...   the last implied positive value would never be reached but the novel would approach "complete negation" *as a limit*   it would be completely negative in effect   in fact, this is the method used by pirandello to prove an "illogical" proposition: 'all explanations of an event are false'

characters attract "accident" while others are immune   wyatt is in
general immune, while otto &   tho he has "substance" like wyatt
    stanley arent   the caricatured characters are confronted with
every variety of "accident"   mr pivner is diabetic—does hartman
even know pivners a comic character?—but its *impossible* in the terms
of the book that wyatt could get diabetes   thus in *the recognitions*
"giving oneself shots" of insulin isnt absurd per se but because only
absurd characters would have to

pivner suffers a totally absurd false arrest, wyatt evades arrest as a
matter of course:

> —I don't know, I don't know, I don't know where the police are. I
> know that two of them were taking me somewhere afterwards and I
> got away from them . . . and came here. How should I know where
> the police are? Why should I . . . care where the police are.

(p685)   pivners twisted & turned by whatever anyone says to him,
wyatts unaffected by esthers constantly trying to get at him, he doesnt
defend himself or answer but goes on with what he was saying   hartmans false premise is that in the novel, as in real life, almost anyone
could have an accident, get diabetes, slip on a banana peel   he
might as well attack kafkas *metamorphosis* because a man cant turn
into a bug   "—I said to him, if you really believed what you wrote
there, you'd be morally obliged to blow your brains out" (an absurd
person in *the recognitions,* 614)   "Surely it is disturbing to find a
book which is potentially so very fine but whose method of attitude is
calculated deliberately to exclude us" (hartman)

youre in it, buddy!

a 2d ambiguity is that doing the opposite is no remedy for being
absurd   (ie pivner giving up shots for shock)   its what the comic
characters in the book are always trying, but their way of being the
opposite partakes of their absurd nature & backfires   otto counter-
acts what he thinks is his uninteresting nothingness with romantic lies
about himself   no one listens   when pivner uses dale carnegies
methods it only makes it more obvious that he cant win friends or
influence people   it wouldnt be in character for him to refuse insulin, but if a more rebellious caricature did hed still be a caricature

negative cliche: what! no resolution?

the recognitions has no happy ending   hollywood overdoses have
weakened the demand for lastpage euphoria, even berger demands
only "a clue to the way out"

> he explores extensively the possibilities of religion in our time. But
> his alternative is far less clear than his indictment, and this be-
> comes an extremely pessimistic novel. (stocking)

(tho lightened by "often hilarious" portraits)   do novelists have to
cure the world?

> Everything in the book ends in death or destruction, the end of the
> road for nihilism. (laycock)

what does life end in?   hartmans too sophisticated to use the cliche
without apology   so he uses it *with* apology, whats the difference?

I will say that the creation of the minister is nothing short of
wonderful, and that that of his son is even better. I wish only that
Mr. Gaddis had stuck more closely to these people, as centralizing
devices if nothing else, and not depended instead on the divergent
density of his writing to provide a center we can cling to. In that
case he might have been able to work out some sort of resolution—
or whatever you want to call it: an *ending,* perhaps—which might
have enabled us to see this book as a true novel and not a brilliant
but diffuse polemic.

a counterfeit sentence   the non seq couldnt have been really a con-
dition for hartmans approval, he lies when he says it could   like
when he says if the real ambiguity of gaddis position—"whatever it
is"—had been fully stated "we might have had here a book we could
consider side by side with the very best"   a fake if & a fake then

simak too starts apologizing for dragging in this old wornout cliche:

the one objection which sticks in this reviewer's craw—and it is not
by any means a legitimate criticism, but simply a matter of personal
prejudice

but gets brasher

—is that while indictment after indictment is trotted out and the
evidence set up, the world convicted and all but sentenced, not one
ray of hope is held forth for an escape from This Terrible Mess in
which we find outselves [sic]. The one glimmer that we can find, and
there is nothing to indicate that the author meant it so, is that we
might be better off if we went back to the old paganism of 2,000
years ago.

because he simaks learned the value of humility   if you seem to
laugh at yourself as well as your victim it shows youre modest & the
readers more likely to believe whatever nonsense youre peddling.
like the disgusting capital letters in "This Terrible Mess"

the grimmest work of art   being really there   can give the possibility of specific hopes   critics prefer commercial trash, literary
painkiller that promises much more but delivers nothing

in westerns & mysteries, the happy ending & invulnerable hero trick
has a social result   it reinforces peoples belief that somehow they
wont suffer growing old & being brutally wounded & smashed in dying.
so they read the world as a novel, theres great apparently unavoidable
danger—but everything will be all right   every time, *this* war scare
cant be it   since the bombs cant appear in the last chapter they
believe its all right to help build them

rolo says *the recognitions* "theme is familiar—the modern world is hell."
the "resolution of his theme of damnation" is in wyatts last scenes.
but the resolution "is presented too thinly and too obscurely to
emerge as a counterpoint to the thunderous chorus of perdition."
should get all the way to purgatory?   rolos own review has exactly
the strong fake resolution he demands of gaddis!   *the recognitions*

is "a somewhat incoherent semi-failure" & *also* "one of the half dozen most remarkable first novels published by American writers since the end of the nineteen-thirties"   he puts the kind words last so by the rules of the review racket its a "favorable review"   if hed put them 1st it would have been *un*favorable

| rolo's last 2 paras | rolo reversed |
| (favorable review) | (unfavorable review) |

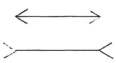

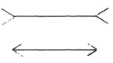

The novel's central failure is that the characters through whom the corruption of the modern world is dramatized are inadequate for the purpose. Too many of them are drawn from Bohemia, which has always been (along with better things) the refuge of fakers, self-deceivers, and hysterics. One does not convincingly demonstrate that the world is insane by describing life in an insane asylum.

A second failing is that the theme has been elaborated before the halfway mark and what follows is further illustration rather than development. As for the resolution, it is presented too thinly and too obscurely to emerge as a counterpoint to the thunderous chorus of perdition. There are other obscurities, some of them due to excessive deployment of the author's phenomenal erudition; and generally speaking, Mr. Gaddis has been mastered by, and not achieved mastery over, the delirium he wishes to depict. In spite of these flaws, which make *The Recognitions* a somewhat incoherent semi-failure, the book seems to me one of the half dozen most remarkable first novels published by American writers since the end of the nineteen-thirties. A work of 956 pages in the nightmarish vein could easily sink into unbearable dreariness; but as far as this reader was concerned, *The Recognitions* retained a quality of excitement to the end. Mr. Gaddis has wit and passion and imagination in abundance, as well as seriousness and learning.

A work of 956 pages in the nightmarish vein could easily sink into unbearable dreariness; but as far as this reader was concerned, *The Recognitions* retained a quality of excitement to the end. Mr. Gaddis has wit and passion and imagination in abundance, as well as seriousness and learning. A profound sense of irony enables him to distill savage comedy and atrocious farce out of his doomsday vision of the world. His extravagant portraiture is arresting and frequently brilliant. All this adds up to something new in contemporary American fiction—a highbrow novel of ideas which has the qualities which our intellectual novels have tended to lack: momentum, range, and imaginative vitality. In spite of these virtues, which make the book seem to me one of the half dozen most remarkable first novels published by American writers since the end of the nineteen-thirties, *The Recognitions* is a somewhat incoherent semi-failure. The novel's central failure is that the characters through whom the corruption of the modern world is dramatized are inadequate for the purpose. Too many of them are drawn from Bohemia, which has always been (along with better things) the refuge of fakers, self-deceivers, and hysterics. One does not convincingly demonstrate that the world is insane by describing life in an insane asylum.

A second failing is that the theme has been elaborated before the halfway mark and what

rolo (cont.)	rolo reversed (cont.)

A profound sense of irony enables him to distill savage comedy and atrocious farce out of his dooms-day vision of the world. His extravagant portraiture is arresting and frequently brilliant. All this adds up to something new in contemporary American fiction—a highbrow novel of ideas which, flawed though it is, has the qualities which our intellectual novels have tended to lack: momentum, range, and imaginative vitality.

follows is further illustration rather than development. As for the resolution, it is presented too thinly and too obscurely to emerge as a counterpoint to the thunder-ous chorus of perdition. There are other obscurities, some of them due to excessive deployment of the author's phenomenal erudition; and generally speaking, though his work has many virtues, Mr. Gaddis has been mastered by, and not achieved mastery over, the delirium he wishes to depict.

negative cliche: "just everybody"

hartman's Big Lie, that *the recognitions* is only absolute negation, against *only everything*   snyder sees it isnt:

> It does not say that everything is phony and that all artists are forgers, but it does show clearly that many people prefer the imitation to the original in art.

but others grab the chance to exaggerate:

> GADDIS' real intent, however, after forcing things and people into alternative strait jackets, is to equate everything with the bad (mccarthy)

> Mr. Gaddis seems to be saying that there is nothing good, true or beautiful in modern life, but his view of modern life is too restricted to be meaningful. (burnette)

> Obviously, Mr. Gaddis is angry at fakery—religious, literary, artistic; indeed one is inclined to suspect that he regards all of western culture (which he has apparently made an enormous effort to assimilate) as one huge fraud. (swados)

> If you have a mind as brilliant and depraved as that of the author of this novel you can make all love, all learning, all science, all art and all religion counterfeit. (north)

> "The Recognitions" presents life as a huge forgery (morse)

> We have lost everything, Gaddis seems to say, and so we are all lost! He sees no virtue in anything (smith)

> life in the twentieth century, viewed with negative bias against a backdrop of our whole cultural history and adjudged a tissue of lies and pretense at all levels of society and of perception. (dawedeit)

would she say "positive bias"?   bass has the true frightened spite:

> Why has Mr. Gaddis taken such pains to detail the doings of these forgers and the recognitions of these doings? He is obviously

disgusted with the modern world and its phonies and its jerks and
its advertising men and its rich people and its poor people and just
everybody. He takes a smack at everything and everybody in the
manner of Eliot and Joyce and Cummings, but they do it much
better and much, much shorter.

FIRE jackson for building his review on this lie:

> what the author is after is not so much to tell a direct, clear story as
> to show the reader in his own special mirror that today's world (so
> runs the author's belief) is uniformly corrupt, venal, silly, frequently
> evil, and everlastingly at least half-fake.
> Now, of course it would be futile to debate this with Mr. Gaddis.
> The novelist is privileged to select the segment of life he wants to
> illuminate and to say what he wants about it—even to declare that
> his picture is the whole picture.

jackson "balances" with 1 weight   the concession he just made he
soon retracts   indiangiving—its a good way to pad a review

> To return to the author's reflection of a world, well, it was Edmund
> Burke who admitted he didn't know how to draw up an indictment
> against a whole people, and Mr. Gaddis is in the same predicament,
> except that one is by no means sure he knows it as Burke did.

but jackson *is* sure gaddis does *not* know it:

> His indictment against one segment of our society has truth,
> force, a vicious bite often. In essence, it says, as one of his charac-
> ters puts it, "People react. That's all they do now, react; they've
> reacted until it's the only thing they can do, and finally there's no
> room for anyone to do anything but react."*
> This is a true-bill, within the limits of the special segment of
> society the author studies. It is true, even, to some extent beyond
> those limits. But the catch is in the word "people," and therefore in
> the statement his whole novel makes. This means, flatly, "all
> people," and it won't do. As Burke knew, there is no method of
> indicting everybody. The attempt is bound to fall of its own—in this
> case excessive—weight.

wyatt's "People" means, flatly, of course, & obviously, "most people".
not "all people"   see p143   *the recognitions* taken as indictment
indicts "most people"   its hartmans lie again, a refuge for phonies
who can hide behind "we cant *all* be phony"

the *time* hack   or hack pack   sets up a shocking gaddisview so
he can cut it down to size as patriotism demands:

> As Author Gaddis sees it, the 20th century U.S. is a soggy butt
> end of western civilization, an age of publicity and duplicity in which
> the phonies have inherited the earth. Pronouncing a scarcely
> original, but nevertheless grandiose, anathema

(would *time* have praised the very 1st unamerican for his "originality"?)
cut down to size by projection, the *time* hacks frivolous with his phony
phrase "literary specialists in damnation" so "Author Gaddis" must be
unserious too

---

the recognitions 143   misquoted

But Author Gaddis also intends *The Recognitions* as a spiritual rebuke ("I wonder, when I step out of doors, how the past can tolerate us"). Unfortunately, the best he can do for a symbol of evil is to trade in Melville's white whale for Manhattan's Madison Avenue. Like other literary specialists in damnation, William Gaddis has held a seashell to his ear and convinced himself that just about all humanity is drowning.

gaddis novel can hardly be classified as just another expose of the admen   but *time* classifies on, its "books" section should be re-named "literary fashions"   its job: supplying cocktail chitchat to the superficial

negative cliche: "bizarre characters"

walk your eyes from madisonavenue to greenwich village   (stopping off in church: "Mr. Gaddis' novel ["an overwhelming nightmare"], shrouded in mysticism, lacks the leavening which a few sane, normal characters would have given it" (mcalister))   take the following as a "negative" sociological hypothesis for which the rest of the novel (or textbook as some of the critics seem to think) must supply "convincing demonstration":

Tragedy was foresworn, in ritual denial of the ripe knowledge that we are drawing away from one another, that we share only one thing, share the fear of belonging to another, or to others, or to God; love or money, tender equated in advertising and the world, where only money is currency, and under dead trees and brittle ornaments prehensile hands exchange forgeries of what the heart dare not surrender.

(*the recognitions* 103)   dawedeit says: "THIS LOFTY statement is acted out by a large, but not really representative, cross-section" mostly persons involved with the arts or religion   not enough "bour-geois characters"   too much "satire of Greenwich Village eccen-trics"   gaddis doesnt know "the wide world" well & his "brilliant pyrotechnics may, then, cast little light on the terrain that most of us travel"

dixon: gaddis lays bare "a world of counterfeiters and forgers"   "a cynical work, but with one saving grace: Chances are the reader will not see himself in these pages. The characters are strictly Greenwich Village"

livingston: gaddis "judgment of the world today" "shockingly lacks coverage of many positive values"   he may correctly describe "a small percentage of society" "prototypes of Greenwich Village circa 1920"   but "as an all-encompassing view" his "devastating picture" is inadequate to "many of the virtues of this civilization"—"he omitted the great bulk of the American populace"

price: every "phase of modern civilization" is "cast aside with burning contempt" by gaddis   he may be "frightfully accurate" about the "loveless world" of his novel, many of whose people "were weaned intellectually in Greenwich Village"   but he includes neither "the Midwestern farmer who loves the land and his family, nor the clerk, nor

the factory worker, each attempting to meet his problems and provide
for his family with such fortitude as he may possess"   "Thus in using
only one side of the coin, perhaps Gaddis, too, is guilty of a bit of
counterfeiting"*

rolo: to dramatize "the corruption of the modern world" bohemians are
inadequate   "One does not convincingly demonstrate that the world
is insane by describing life in an insane asylum"

its not the purpose of fiction to tell the truth not *the* purpose   but a
good novelist wont tell the same crude lies about people that are
believed all around him   each lie exposed reveals a truth & so
novelists   unlike sociologists   *do* do sociology, tell what people
are really like   its a byproduct & has nothing to do with whether a
novelist is "realistic"   kafka uncovered as much as zola

the novel as an effective instruments about a century old   in this
time novelists have uncovered perhaps a *twentieth* of the terrible truth
about people   the reason is, you cant write a novel from what you
know   you have to have felt it, & those who feel what the world is
really like are soon in madhouses—its intolerable

the surface view we have most of the time, the one that seems
obvious & everyday, of man as more or less all right, is false   to
know what kind of wars are now going to be fought, with what
weapons & how they get to be used, is to know the world   the same
contrast between the civilized 9to5 life in a government office or
laboratory & the crimes that are prepared there   between the button-
pusher & the bomb   is the contrast between the public face of the
adjusted citizen & *his* crimes   hes ready to take his assigned part in
destroying the enemy across the world & he rehearses with daily
mutilations of his family & himself

the voter, childtorturer & future killer in whatever cause his government offers him is as much a biological & social misfit as any "bizarre
characters" (burnette) in *the recognitions*   the latter, to be sure,
arent overburdened with mates, jobs, children   with roots, dull roles
—and *masks,* public impersonal masks   (see the married couple in
public!   & see them alone)

the recognitions after all is far, far more interesting than real life.
more happens faster & sharper   even "Greenwich Village eccen-
trics" need lots of whittling to enter the book without slowing it down
to tedium   imagine then, if youve read the book, an irruption of midwestern farmers who love the land, clerks & factoryworkers providing
gelt for their loved ones with the utmost fortitude   what a bore! how
could they fit in?   theyd have to be rolled in the gutter a hundred
pages just to get the mask off   by the time they belonged in the
book theyd be "bizarre" too   you might as well try to jam them into
gulliver's travels or *ulysses*

if novels are reserpine the characters should be pleasant folk, if not it
doesnt matter   its true if only the weird are corrupt the corruption of

*of a textbook, or guidebook?   *the recognitions* is "Baedeker's *Babel*" (475)
not baedekers *usa*   cf simak "loaded evidence" & proof "by showing only the
one side of the coin"

72

recognitions characters doesnt represent the real majority world   but thats not why 5 critics hit on the same point independently (yes, this time!) & argued it long & strong   they did protest too much

characters

the critics fail to know the characters in *the recognitions*   who're described mostly in terms of what they *do* not what they *are*   most critics mentioning wyatt describe him mainly or only as a painter who forges old masters (blurb):

> Gwyon's mixed-up son, Wyatt, who paints a pseudo-Flemish master-piece (chitty 9/9/62)

but the points not that wyatt forges art but what forging does to him (& its more than "forging")

wyatt is *not* the "chief symbol of despair" or "the overriding symbol of fraudulence" (bloom, bradley) or "rather like Kafka's 'K'" (highet) or "doomed and damned" (north) or "turns to forging old masters to earn a living" (simak) or "mad"/"demented" (stocking, *u s quarterly book review*)   he doesnt cease "to have a personality" "a third of the way through" (coldwell)

burnette's "Wyatt is an unsympathetic character" is worth quoting. by black magic *time* presents wyatt as a *typical young artist:*

> On the follow-the-hero level, the action of *The Recognitions* may seem simple. Wyatt Gwyon is the shy son of a New England preacher. His mother has died during a trip to Spain, and he is brought up under the gimlet eye and Puritan maxims of a crabby maiden aunt. In Paris, he holes up in a studio and paints, but he gets panned by the critics. Wyatt is soon back in a Greenwich Village flat with a draftsman's job and a possessive wife just out of analysis.* He sheds his wife, and sells himself into esthetic and moral bondage forging "undiscovered" Flemish masterpieces for a millionaire dealer in expensive fakes. This work drives him to the fringes of sanity and murder. Fleeing the U.S., he makes an obscurely redemptive pilgrimage to his mother's grave in Spain.

(note the reductions to the classify-&-generalize level: "shy son" "crabby maiden aunt" "holes up in a studio" "Greenwich Village flat" (it isnt) "possessive wife" etc)   berger's the only critic to connect wyatt with "less emphasis on self-consciousness"

critics on other characters are usually brief & uninspired, or blurb-inspired   "an American musician" (laycock) hardly describes stanley, nor should he be classed (with wyatt) among the "forgers" "phonies" & "hypocrites" (parke)   gwyon's no "Puritan parent" (powell), & "wonderful religious dad" wont do either (coleman 9/11/62)   esme gets very little comment (because shes not mentioned in the blurb?)   better no comment that rolo's:

> an artist's model with a face of Madonna-like purity and the mind of an imbecilic child—a child who has discovered that heroin is more

---

*to put it mildly! (*the recognitions* 80)

comforting than thumb-sucking

or livingston on aunt may:

> Nowhere in the novel is there a man or woman (with the possible exception of the aunt) who draws from the past religious history which Mr. Gaddis so eloquently describes enough of the positive to live a good, Christian life.

(she & mr pivner being the "only semihonest characters" ie the only squares)   rugoff finds the use of primary characters in depth *and* caricatures an "exasperating mélange" "of shrewd and of merely grotesque characterization"*   bloom: the "characters are fragmented thoughts, disembodied voices" "they can't be regarded as persons"   powell calls them "desperately indistinguishable from each other"—shes exactly wrong as usual   & the library of congress hack:

> the narrator's contempt for his characters keeps him outside their imaginations, so that some are no more than names.

an outstanding feature of *the recognitions* is how sharp & easily distinguishable the minor characters are   some appear often, some a few times but sharply, & shading off further a few are merely named or appear so briefly you have little idea who they are, as often happens in real life   these cause a few dull lines but theyre *not* the ones the library of congress man means & their use has nothing to do with contempt

the critics did an especially lousy job on the characters   mostly seeming to be writing about some other book   & the characters are usually what distinguish a great novel from an ordinary one

plot

1 rushed reading of *the recognitions* makes hash of the plot   which some rapidreading students found "irritatingly opaque" (*time*) or even nonexistent:

> Plot does not exist (bloom)

> a novel without a defined plot (kirkus)

> not, strictly speaking, a story at all, but an immense canvas filled with shifting pictures (morse)

> a sprawled giant of a book, with little plot but a great deal to say. (demarest)

> Structurally it is a series of symbolic episodes calculated not to tell a story but to suggest the sterility of contemporary life. (rugoff)

> the story shifts from continent to continent through a maze of interlocking plots and a veritable forest of symbol and allegory without ever assuming a skeletal outline of real substance. (bradley)

---

*if its different it must be "merely"

a careless 1st reader of *war & peace* might forget who the characters are & lose the storyline each time its interrupted by tolstoy remarks on history   if he dared to write a review at this point itd be like jackson's who got derailed by the caricature sections in gaddis book:

> There is small use trying to outline any plot in so diffuse a book. There is a vague narrative line

> But this story-thread keeps disappearing like a swimmer with cramps in the ocean of brilliantly drawn phonies that Mr. Gaddis' fertile imagination creates.

snyder mysteriously judges that "time and place have little importance" in the story   in desbarats' fantasy the camera may have discouraged authors from attempting the novel proper   "stories can be told, through television and movies, more effectively in dramatic form, as they were in Shakespeare's time"   by who, chayefsky?   can greshams law connect the audience of tens of millions with the one of tens of thousands?   if not, the dishonest tv stories cant drive out the honest novels

> Gaddis tells us not only a story but what he thinks of it.
> Maybe this obviates plot in the conventional sense. (desbarats)

maybe not!   you should shun the quoteprecis of *the recognitions* in #10 of *newspaper* & buy the book instead, but my digest does show that gaddis has a clear storyline/lines   his storyline has much the same function as in most novels, including realistic ones & all the above comments are from fools   bass, taking the opposite suspicion, is just as wrong:

> Every character in the book had drowned along the way, dragged down by the weight of his words and the plot treadmill upon which he was forced to operate.

plus

some things the 55 original critics said with moderate or better insight & competence   (not all favorable nor do i agree with them all). berger (see p72 above)   bloom: "the conflict between deception and recognition" (& p60 above)   bradley: "his humor the kind that slaps you full in the face half a dozen pages after you have passed it by". cahoon: "manages, without mention of war or the atomic bomb, to chronicle and dissect important aspects of contemporary society"; "A vast panorama of interlocking plots and recurring phrases and symbols has been carefully organized into a novel of dimension and power". coldwell: "It is only recognition of deception that can make a man real". conroy: "considerably more than a tour de force or an exercise in scholastic, technical and rhetorical virtuosity. Its essentially earnest examination of certain maladies of postwar society is both terrifying and disturbing"   corrington: "A novel like William Gaddis' 'The Recognitions' manages to separate the mature critical mind from that of the opinionated amateur who would attempt to protect 'custom' or 'the American way' or any similar fantasy from the uncompromising scrutiny it deserves"; "we cannot deny the validity of what he has created from the veiled shame of a world without faith or love" (& deflates the "balancing" trick p60 above)   dawedeit: "Recognition of patterns plays a major role in the book's design. Structurally, it combines the classic, vertical form of organization with the horizontal 'slice of life,' in alternating episodes. To this frame both long and wide, Gaddis adds a third dimension through an intricate system of historical, literary, artistic, musical and religious allusion. He has used many of these as symbols, or leit motifs, threading them through the novel to splice the horizontal and vertical beams" (& p9 above)   demarest: "a galactic gallery of characters, some of whom it is hard to keep track of, but which range from biting caricatures to studies in depth"; "the author's zeal for unmasking fraud makes it hard to distinguish Stanley's genuine faith from the account executive's 'smart' conversion"; "this is, like *Ulysses,* a book which has emerged from other books, a product as much of reading as living"; "But it is also in spite of its faults (which are the only worthwhile ones of trying to say too much, achieve the impossible) a genuine and personal book, *sui generis*" (italics: boldface)   desbarats (p60 above)   mccarthy: "Wyatt, the son, a man who can neither find nor lose himself"; knows its camilla whos "canonized" (& p52 above)   powell: wyatt "oblivious to love and evil and therefore used by both"   price: knows recktall brown a symbol of mephistopheles (& p48 above)   rogers: "The novel pictures a Bedlam, not a place of pure, clean madness, however, but mean and petty. Indeed the novel itself is a Bedlam irresistibly fascinating; you can't take your eyes off it, or your mind from it"   snyder (p68 above). wharton: "Unlike that of 'Ulysses' the inspiration seems Roman rather than Hellenic"; "some writers of our day who search the past for nuggets of eloquence, as if to store them up against the Dark Ages they subconsciously await"   yeiser: "The novel may have some literary ancestors. If so, they are not easily recognizable. One thinks first of 'Ulysses,' for several reasons, which are more apparent than real"

17 critics, 29 quotes—pitiful!   & what the list lacks in quantity it doesnt make up in quality   a mediocre crew

the 2 competent reviews were by cahoon* & rogers, both strongly favorable—as were corrington & stevens (& wagner who didnt read the book)   really minus reviews were by geismar (& nonreaders wagenknecht & the *toronto globe & mail* hack) & perhaps berger**

1 of the most favorable reviews was one of the worst   don stevens' insincere puff in the *worcester telegram*—a typical jargonized "rave" review & not a response to *the recognitions* at all   his 1st para:

Such a strikingly brilliant and major work as this necessitates a reviewer's throwing his hat in the air—he has nowhere else to put it, having lost his head in the intoxication of finding a book of such magnitude and power.

*for the *library journal*—a bunch of cheap crooks!   on the copy of the review they sent the publisher was a form request for a bribe: "A LIBRARY JOURNAL review in the MAR 15 1955 issue. Achieve the sales potential implicit in this review by advertising in the next possible issue"

**relatively favorable (by my application of *book review digest* standards): key #s 8 11 12 13 16 17 28 39 46 50 62 68 71 83 84 85   relatively unfavorable: 3 9 18 35 40 52 53 56 78   noncommittal: twentyone reviews alexander woollcott lives!   stevens did a little corroborative reading but mostly steals from the blurb:

stevens	*recognitions* blurb
across the big-as-life canvas, move a score of figures. they pursue their own desired deceptions.	Scores of characters move back and forth within the design, each one busy in pursuing his own desired deception.
Wyatt, who forges the paintings of Old Masters	Wyatt, is a painter who forges Old Masters
Mr. Sinisterra, a counterfeiter	Mr. Sinisterra is a honest-to-God counterfeiter
Valentine, the art critic	Basil Valentine, the corrupt and corrupting art critic
Mrs. Deigh, the literary agent	Agnes Deigh, the distracted literary agent
Otto, the playwright	Otto, the vain young playwright
Anselm, the poet	Anselm, the acne-ridden poet
For the pattern of forgery is shown to be emotional and spiritual, as well as actual—and gaining momentum each time the world discards the genuine for the paste-copy.	The pattern of forgery, emotional and spiritual as well as actual a world in which the genuine is continually being discarded in favor of a successful facsimile.
He's sure to shock and anger as many as he captivates, but he should welcome the storm of controversy	Readers may be shocked, or angered, or frightened a thesis and a point of view which cannot escape being controversial

quoting from the blurb without credits not rare*   the whole *louisville courier-journal* notice was stolen from the blurb   favorite blurbphrase was "pattern of forgery, emotional and spiritual as well as actual" (plagiarized by burnette corrington klein & stevens)   FIRE them all for theft

after the 1st round

in the years after the 55 reviews there were some more mentions of *the recognitions,* mostly favorable   w g rogers twice more (4/55: *new world writing* "may sometime have reason to be proudest of having printed a chapter from William Gaddis' extraordinary novel". 12/18/55: "Gaddis' overpowering first novel")

---

*one reviewer wrote me that when i object to this i only arbitrarily "set up" my "own ground-rules"   he might also argue that the more a critic steals from the blurb the less room for boners of his own

in the *saturday review* spring fiction poll *the recognitions* got a surprising 4 votes (bradley, a d emmart of the *baltimore sun,* carl victor little of the *houston press,* yeiser) tying for 3d place*   & in the years-best poll 2 votes (emmart, yeiser) tying for 4th place   (note in a poll there are no votes *against*)

*newsweek*s yearend sumup found gaddis book "too experimental in style to compete" (in sales) with other long books such as kantor's *andersonville* (which won the 2d *saturday review* poll with 14 votes). *time's* survey was 1st to criticize the critics, tho inaccurately ("Some critics uneasily and unjustly ignored it")

john w aldridge (*in search of heresy*) attacked the critics intelligently, using gaddis novel & harrington's *the revelations of doctor modesto* as objectlessons

in 1957 anthony west listed *the recognitions* as 1 of 25 great books from world literature ("the most interesting and remarkable novel written by a young American in the last twenty-five years. It will one day take a place in classic American literature beside the work of Thomas Wolfe as an expression of the developing American spirit")

1958: gerald walker ("often obscure but always brilliant") in a *ny times* review of another novel   1959: eugene mcnamara ("packed with truth so real as to punch the breath out of one") in *the critic*   gilbert highet, whose original review called it "a pity that" gaddis "spiritual conflicts have apparently been too intense to allow him to produce a truly effective work of art" improved his opinion a la hicks, shelving the book where his "few private novels crouch and look up hopefully, like delicate animals caught in a burning forest, or else sail gallantly away, on wings of courage and imagination, into the past from which they came"!   what an ass   1960: charles monaghan in *commonweal* listed *the recognitions* among "some of the finest writing of recent times"   1962: mcnamara again discussed gaddis, as 1 of 4 american writers seeming to him "to be creating works which are original in a radical sense"

in 7 years, not much action   for "gaddis underground" work in these years a coup by david markson was unsurpassed & indeed unsurpassable   his *epitaph for a tramp* came out as a 25c paperback original in 1959   its a privateeye potboiler—the worst   on p27-8 he works in some gaddisian "forged conversation" at a bar, with an in-joke about "willie"   i should explain that at this point the eye is trailing the "tramp," ie his wife   he finds her naked on the bed of a college kids pad in greenwich village   he orders the kid into the toilet & tells off his wife   while he waits for her to dress some description is called for, what such an apt looks like, stolen noparking sign, label on expensive jacket dad paid for, sheet of paper in typewriter—interrupted essay for comparative lit—on it the kid has typed:

And thus it is my conclusion that The Recognitions *by William Gaddis is not merely the best American first novel of our time, but*

---

*raymond walters jr   prefacing & rejoicing as "Fiction Makes a Comeback" remarked of the fiction books voted for that "while none of them is likely to make Hemingway or Faulkner look to his laurels, they offer rewarding reading for the spring months ahead"

perhaps the most significant single volume in all American fiction since Moby Dick, *a book so broad in scope, so rich in comedy and so profound in symbolic inference that—*

the 2d round

the meridian paperback of *the recognitions* came out late march 1962. john d seelye strongly recommended it in the *berkeley gazette*   i somehow managed to get #12 out in feb   & as a protest vs publishers' advertising budgets took a page ad for the novel in the *village voice*   this caused a lot of talk in the village, mainly wondering who bribed me   barkham sounded the 2 motifs of the 2d round (saturday review syndicate): "unjustly neglected" & "deserves the wider audience it will now receive"   the *ny times* failed to get with it, just had a para quoting hicks 1955 con*   dolbier's *ny herald tribune* review was very favorable ("its reappearance as a paperback is more than welcome") & admitted 1955 was "one of American criticism's weakest hours"   however, the book did *not* appear 12 yrs ago—& its not 976 pp long

i had lunch with meridians publicity director & the literary gossip-columnist jerome beatty jr   beattys not interested in books so while eating the free food i expended a years supply of charm & told every scandalous anecdote about my personal life i could think of   this worked beautifully & there was a long *saturday review* account of my peculiarities, *newspaper* & a plug for *the recognitions* that bordered on the serious

now there was a burst of publicity (the "gaddis underground story"). hayes' *new haven register* review started "One of the most remark-able—and most neglected—American novels of the 1950's"   he forgot to tell his readers that over 80% of the review was his old 1955 review wordforword   hogan's *sf chronicle* column was gossip a la beatty   then the *ny times* surrendered, they cant bear to miss a story so their gossipcolumn had a para too, about *the recognitions* being revived everywhere   newquist's *chicago star* review was plus. saal in the *saturday review* was quite unlike geismar in 1955: "at last receiving proper recognition" "immensely talented"

1 morning i got a phonecall from the literary gossipcolumnist (soon theyll replace reviewers entirely) martha macgregor of the *ny post*   i tried to wake up but soon realized she wasnt much interested either. i feebly denied the accusation that i might have "constructive advice" for critics & went back to sleep   she wrote:

> "Book news is so polite," complains a reader. Hoping for some im-polite news, I called Jack Green, who has attacked 53 critics as "bastards" for their reviews of William Gaddis' "The Recognitions" back in 1955. But Mr. Green was disappointingly courteous. Not one four-letter word, not a single "slob," "thief," "fake," or "imbecile."

---

*they were busy preparing the book coup of the year   in may the *times* was actually able to locate a novelist whod write a favorable review of herman wouk's *youngblood hawke*   (commercial antisexual filth!)   to go with the 2p ad in the same issue   (im proud to say i instantly   reading wouks 1st novel *aurora dawn*   spotted him as the worst writer in the world)

if i had only known what she wanted!   *publishers' weekly* had a
beattylike column ("A NOVEL with seven years' worth of underground
reputation is beginning to see daylight in a big way"), reported sales of
"a comfortable 200-copy weekly average, with business particularly
strong in college towns"   w g rogers' *ny herald tribune* review (with
editors note derived from *publishers' weekly*) was again very plus   so
was arthur sainer's perceptive *village voice* review ("as great a novel
as we have produced in the last sixty years" "Gaddis must be reckoned
not only with Hemingway and Faulkner but with Joyce and Proust and
Mann")

this was my 2d raid into the publicity world   its good for laughs but
leaves that sick feeling   #12 touched a raw nerve, got some action.
the establishment surrendered without a fight, admitting its sins with
humorous tolerance for itself & those who had no right to be right   i
didnt know my writing (that is, my mimeographing) was cute enough to
win such bouquets as "Number One Gaddis Fan" "chief cheerleader"
& "toy newspaper"   nor did i expect one of the "bastards" to ask me
to write a review for his paper!

the recognitions was published in england in september   philip
toynbee's review was very favorable but the other critics were sourly
"balanced"   best boner was chitty in *the sunday telegraph:* stanley
belongs with the plagiarists & tricksters because the music hes playing when the church collapses on him is "copied"

back in the u s: *the recognitions* has moved quite a way toward
acceptance, but the establishments surrender was premature & misleading   most of the 1962 plugs had only a momentary effect
because they were by phonies, insincere jobholders who often hadnt
even read the book   what seelye, rogers, sainer published could
have a real effect because they were writing what they really believed.
more such work is needed

bibliography

william gaddis "le chemin des anes" (draft of section ii, *the recognitions*) *new world writing* (ny: new american library 4/52) 210-22. (mentioned on p35 76 above)
william gaddis *the recognitions* (u s hardcover ed, ny: harcourt, brace & co 3/10/55 $7.50; canadian publisher, toronto: george j mcleod $8.50)

entries include:
key # of entry, F (if to be FIRED), * (if one of 55 original reviews)
author & title, publication, date & page no[*]
(in parentheses, page nos of references to entry in *this* article)
crossreferences to other entries, giving key #s

a.l.a. (*american library association*) *booklist*   (mentioned on p2 above)
1   aldridge, john w *in search of heresy* (ny 1956) 200-1   (p32-3 77 above)
amarillo news see entries #58 59 below
2   american institute of graphic arts *fifty books of the year 1955* (ny 1956) #35   details of physical production of *the recognitions*
arkansas (little rock) *gazette* see #61 below
associated press, see #58 59 60 61
atlanta journal & constitution see #45
atlantic monthly see #62
baltimore sun   (p77 77 above)   see #9 below
3 F* bass, milton r *berkshire eagle* (pittsfield mass) 3/19/55 12. (p17 19 21 21 23 39-40 43 44 52 55 60-1 68-9 74 75 above)
4 F* berger, john *the nation* 4/30/55 376-8   (9-10 12-3 17 27 36 42 43 54 65 72 74 75)   see also #7 below
berkeley gazette see #87
berkshire eagle see #3
5   *best sellers* "index to this volume" 6/15/55 59 60   (37) #35
blackfriars see #47a
6 F* bloom, edward a *providence journal* 3/13/55 vi:vi   (1 4 14-5 17 24 24 41 42 43 60 72 73 73 74)
book of the month club news see #32
7   *book review digest 1955* (ny 1956) 327-8   (3 26 75)   has excerpts from entries #4 10 21 26 29 38 52 62 63 74, lists #20 36 77 79

*[Brackets contain additional bibliographic information unavailable to Green —S.M.]

boston globe see #40
boston herald see #68
8 F* bradley, van allen *chicago news* (& syndicated) 3?/55   (17 42
    52 52 72 73 74 75 77)   #106
9 F* burnette, frances *baltimore sun* 3/13/55 a14   (12 17 43 43
    44-5 52 54 68 70 71 72 76 76)
10 * cahoon, herbert *library journal* 3/15/55 653   (1 56 74 75).
    #7
11 * *cedar rapids gazette* 5/1/55 [3:4]   (75)
    chicago news see #8 106
    chicago star see #101
    chicago sun-times see #13
    chicago tribune see #79
    cincinnati enquirer see #85
    cleveland plain dealer see #59
    cleveland press see #57
12 * coldwell, david *dallas herald* 3?/55   (41 52 72 74 75)
    columbus dispatch see #46
    commonweal see #20 37 48
13 * conroy, jack *chicago sun-times* 3/13/55 3:4   (53 74 75)
14 F* corrington, william *shreveport times* 8/28/55 2f   (11 11 48-9
    60 60 74-5 75 76)
    critic, the see #47
    dallas herald see #12
    dallas news see #41
15 * dawedeit, glendy *washington post & times herald* 3/13/55 e6.
    (9 41 46 47 49 53 68 70 71 75)
16 F* demarest, donald *the news weekly* (mexico city) late 1955? 2b
    4b   (11 41 51 52 53 73 75 75)
17 * desbarats, peter *montreal gazette* 4/23/55 25   (18 21 48 57
    60 74 75 75)
18 F* dixon, george *pittsburgh press* 3/20/55 [5:8]   (18 21 21 44
    54 70 75)
19 dolbier, maurice "the summing-up in books for 1955" *saturday
    review* 12/24/55 11   (11)   #65 94
    emmart, a d   (see p77 77 above)
20 F* fremantle, anne *commonweal* 4/15/55 55-7   (15-7 19 24 32
    36 39 42 43)   #7
21 F* geismar, maxwell *saturday review* 3/12/55 23   (3 17 19 22
    32-4 53 58 58 75 78)   #7
    gilbert, stuart   (22)   see #24 26 88
22 F girson, rochelle, saturday review syndicate (fla newspaper)
    3/20/55 13   (20-1)
    graves, robert, see #24 88 111
23 green, jack *newspaper* #1 12/4/57 5-7 "best novel ever written
    in america", #2 1/28/58 6, #4 7/3/58 5-6, #8 7/19/59 5, #10
    8/31/60, #11 6/3/61 6, #12-14 2/24 8/25 11/10/62   see
    #89 99 below
24 harcourt, brace & co, ad in *ny times* 3/16/55 31   (2)   ex-
    cerpts from #74 below, from gilbert quote in #26 below, from
    #53 59, from graves quote (see #88 below); quotes dan
    wickenden "The strange and mostly rather frightening new
    generation of writers has produced in Mr. Gaddis a strange,
    frightening, but massive and remarkable talent"
25 harcourt, brace & co, catalog listing, before 3/55 21   draft of
    #26 blurb
26 harcourt, brace & co, jacket of *the recognitions* (u s hardcover

ed) 3/10/55   (1 5-8 14 22 33 41 41-2 44 72 72 72 76 76).
#7 above   blurb; quotes stuart gilbert on jacketback THE
RECOGNITIONS "is a vast and devastating picture of the
world the powers-that-be have doomed us to live in; Mr.
Eliot's Waste Land was only a small corner of the wilderness
so observantly and successfully explored by Mr. Gaddis. Such
a work might easily be lugubrious but the author's wit, irony,
and erudition, combined with a rich diversity of subject matter,
make this book fascinating reading; long though it is, even
longer than 'Ulysses,' the interest, like that of Joyce's masterpiece and for very similar reasons, is brilliantly maintained
throughout"
harper's   (p2 above)
hartford courant see #49

27 F* hartman, carl *western review* winter 1956 171-6   (11 19 24
     34 40 42 45 46 47 47 60 61-5 66 68 69)
28 * hayes, e nelson *the progressive* 6/55 40-1   (10 17 47 58 75
     78)   #96
29 F* hicks, granville *ny times* 3/13/55 br6   (3 25 26-32 46 47 47
     78)   #7
30   hicks, granville, rev. of paul goodman's *the empire city* in *satur-
     day review* 5/23/59 20   (17 26 30 46 47 77)
32   hicks, granville (ed.) in *the living novel: a symposium* (ny 1957).
     (27 29 29-30)   #73
32 * highet, gilbert *book of the month club news* midsummer 1955
     8-9   (35 42 46 47 53 57 72 77)
33   highet, gilbert "artistic forgeries (ii)" wqxr network radio talk
     (printed by book of the month club) 1957   (11)
34   highet, gilbert "a personal library" wqxr network radio talk
     (printed by book of the month club) 6/59   (77)
35 F* hill, william b *best sellers* (univ of scranton) 4/15/55 13   (17
     18 21 21 23 37 37 43 46 48 51 53 75)   #5
     houston press   (p77 above)
     hudson review, the see #72
36 F* jackson, joseph henry *san francisco chronicle* 3/17/55 23.
     (17 46 53 55 69 74)   #7
     keene (nh) *sentinel* see #60
37   kennebeck, edwin, rev. of terry southern's *the magic christian*
     in *commonweal* 4/29/60 133   (46)
38 F* *kirkus' service, bulletin from virginia* 2/1/55 93 94   (11 17
     21 21 44 44 44-5 47 51 73)   #7
39 F* klein, francis a (per publisher) *st louis globe-democrat* 3/13/55
     5f   (1 7-8 43 52 53 75 76)
40 * laycock, edward a (per publisher) *boston globe* 3/13/55 72.
     (11 17 19 21 36 45 45 53 54 65 72 75)
     lewiston (ida) *tribune* see #67
     library journal   (75)   see #10
     library of congress, see #77
     little, carl victor   (p77 above)
41 * livingston, myra c *dallas news* 4/3/55 vi:8   (11 11 19 32 40
     48-9 52 53 70 73)
42 F* *louisville courier-journal* 3/27/55 3:8   (6 76)
43   mailer, norman *advertisements for myself* (ny 1959) 472-3.
     gaddis "of good repute"
     manchester nh news see #58 59
44   markson, david *epitaph for a tramp* (ny: dell publishing co
     11/59; also swedish ed) 27-8 29-31   (77-8)

#24 105

60   rogers, w g "books in review" associated press (*keene* (nh)
       sentinel etc) 4?/55   (76)
61   rogers, w g "reviewing the year in arts" associated press (*ar-
       kansas* (little rock) *gazette* 12/18/55 6f etc)   (76)
62   * rolo, charles j *atlantic monthly* 4/55 80-1   (17 39 39 41 53
       54 66-8 71 72 75)   #7
63 F* rugoff, milton *ny herald tribune* 3/13/55 br6   (17 18 40 43 45
       49 52 52 53-4 61 73 73)   #7
       san diego union see #67
       san francisco chronicle see #36 97
       saturday review   (2 3 3 22 23 31)   see #19 21 30 64 65
       67 95 102
64   *saturday review* "*SR*'s spring poll" with intro by raymond walters
       jr 4/9/55 14-5 42-3   (77)
65   *saturday review* "the year's best" 12/17/55 12-3   (77 77).
       #19
       saturday review syndicate, see #22 67 91
       shreveport times see #14
66 F* simak, clifford d *minneapolis tribune* 3/13/55 home & hobby 14.
       (11 11 17 23 34-5 43 52 52 56 66 71 72)
67 F* smith, harrison (president, *saturday review*) saturday review
       syndicate (*lewiston* (ida) *tribune* 3/13/55 society 9, *san diego
       union, toledo blade, victoria* (bc) *colonist* etc)   released for
       3/12/55   (4 11 11 19 22-3 52 53 68)
68   * snyder, marjorie b *boston herald* 3/13/55 1:4   (11 68 74 75
       75)
       spectator, the see #70 116
69 F* stevens, don *worcester telegram* 3/13/55 d7   (11 13-4 18 48
       53 75-6 76)
70   st john-stevas, norman "printers' censorship" *the spectator*
       (london weekly review) 12/9/55 792 794   (36)
       st louis globe-democrat see #39
       st louis post-dispatch see #83
71 F* stocking, david m *milwaukee journal* 3/6/55 5:4   (39 47 52
       52 65 72 75)
       styron, william, see #88 111
72   * swados, harvey *the hudson review* autumn 1955 460-1   (35
       43 48 54 55-6 68)   #88
73   swados, harvey "the image in the mirror" in granville hicks (ed.)
       the living novel: a symposium (ny 1957)   (48)   #31
       tacoma news-tribune see #58
74   * *time* [by Theodore E. Kalem] 3/14/55 112 114   (2 11 17 39
       42 69-70 72 73)   #7 24
75   *time* "books" 12/26/55 62   (17 77)
       toledo blade see #67
76 F* *toronto globe & mail* 4?/55   (1 5 75)
       trace see #92
       tulsa world see #58 59
77   * *u s quarterly book review* (library of congress) 6/55 214-5.
       (24 72 73)   #7
       victoria (bc) *colonist* see #67
       village voice see #89 98 99 107 108
       virginia kirkus' service, see #38
78 F* "b w" *nashville tennesseean* 3?/55   (4 75)
79 F* wagenknecht, edward *chicago tribune* 4/3/55 4:5   (1 5 5 24
       43 50-1 54 75)   #7

80 F* wagner, charles a (london?) *sunday mirror* 3/27/55 7   (8 75)
81   walker, gerald, rev. of richard condon's *the oldest confession* in
           ny times 6/22/58 br18   (77)
         walters, raymond, jr   (see p77 78 above)   #64 93
         washington post & times herald see #15
82   west, anthony "the pleasures of reading" *woman's day* 7/57 3
           32-3 81-2   (17 77)
         western review see #27
83   * wharton, will *st louis post-dispatch* 3/27/55 4b   (11 36 75 75)
84   * white, ellington *richmond times-dispatch* 3/6/55 f5   (12 17
           41 75)
         wickenden, dan, see #24
         woman's day see #82
         worcester telegram see #69
         wqxr network, see #33 34
85   * yeiser, frederick *cincinnati enquirer* 3/13/55 3:6   (11 17 56
           59-60 75 75 77 77)

the 2d round

william gaddis *the recognitions* (u s paperback ed, ny: meridian books
   (world publishing co) late 3/62 $2.75)

86   meridian books (world publishing co) list of "spring 1962 pub-
           lications" 2?/62   "A rediscovered masterpiece, an unjustly
           neglected classic, a book with a numerous underground of
           admirers . . ."
87   seelye, john d *berkeley gazette* 3/16/62   (78 79)
88   meridian books (world publishing co) back cover of *the recogni-
           tions* (u s paperback ed) late 3/62   blurb abridged & slightly
           revised from #26 above; excerpt from gilbert quote in #26;
           quotes william styron "I stand in great awe of Mr. Gaddis's
           erudition, his attempted scope, his vitality, and indeed his
           genuinely superior use of the language. . . . A virtuoso of rare
           charm, especially when he is being funny—which is very
           funny indeed"; excerpt from #72; quotes robert graves "The
           precision of William Gaddis's style is most unusual in his
           generation of writers. And I am astonished that one who
           shows himself so familiar and up-to-date with the mountain of
           filth, perversion, falsity, and boredom revealed in *The Recog-
           nitions*, should have managed to keep his head clear and his
           heart warm, and his report readable"
89   green, jack, ad for *the recognitions* & #12 of *newspaper* in
           village voice 3/29/62 8   (78)   #23
90   meridian books (world publishing co) *the meridian* spring 1962
           3 4
91   barkham, john, saturday review syndicate 1962   (78)
92   *trace* "the chronicle" spring 1962 99   note on #12 of *news-
           paper*
93   walters, raymond, jr *ny times* 4/8/62 br14   (78)
94   dolbier, maurice *ny herald tribune* 4/14/62 6   (78)   #19
95   beatty, jerome, jr "trade winds" *saturday review* 4/21/62 8-9.
           (78 78 79)
96   hayes, e nelson *new haven register* 4/22/62   (78)   #28
97   hogan, william *san francisco chronicle* 4/26/62 [41]   (78)
98   wilcock, john "the village square" *village voice* 5/3/62 2.

        #107   on #12 of *newspaper*

99   green, jack "letters to the editor" *village voice* 5/10/62 4.
        #23   on #98 above

100   nichols, lewis "in and out of books" *ny times* 5/13/62 br8.
        (78)

101   newquist, roy *chicago star* (& syndicated in los angeles)
        5/13/62   (78)

102   saal, rollene w *saturday review* 5/19/62 40   (78)

103   macgregor, martha "the week in books" *ny post* 5/20/62 m11.
        (78-9)

104   *publishers' weekly* "paperbacks" 6/4/62 94   (79 79)

105   rogers, w g (& editor's note by irita van doren) *ny herald
        tribune* 7/29/62 books 8   (79 79)   #59

106   bradley, van allen "bookman's week" *chicago news* 10/6/62
        18   #8   on #12-13 of *newspaper*

107   wilcock, john "the village square" *village voice* 10/18/62 2.
        #98   mentions #109 below

108   sainer, arthur *village voice* 11/1/62 11 14   (79 79)

william gaddis *the recognitions* (british hardcover ed, london: macgibbon & kee 9/10/62 30 shillings)

109   toynbee, philip *the* (london) *observer weekend review* 9/9/62.
        (79)   "among, to set one's sights vaguely at the right ele-
        vation, the dozen most impressive novels in English which
        have appeared since the war"

110   chitty, susan *the* (london) *sunday telegraph* 9/9/62   (72 79).
        "pretentious. . . . Mr. Gaddis can write and if he'd come off
        the 'Ulysses' act he might be good"

111   macgibbon & kee, blurb of *the recognitions* (british ed) 9/10/62.
        "First published in New York in 1955, *The Recognitions* has
        acquired a growing reputation as one of the key novels of
        our time. It has done this in a curiously 'subterranean' way.
        Its first critics were baffled, if not downright hostile. Since
        1955, groups of readers have discovered the book and their
        admiration has led to much re-thinking about the scope and
        merits of the book. To many young Americans, it is the
        Ulysses of the age (indeed the *New Yorker's* first review
        contained the singularly fatuous comment that the novel
        was like *Ulysses* but not as good . . .).* Among the first
        admirers of the book were William Styron and Robert
        Graves. William Gaddis lives in New York and, so far, *The
        Recognitions* is his only book"

112   coleman, john *the queen* (london weekly women's mag) 9/11/
        62   (72)   "arrogantly presumes that its readers will
        come to it prepared to examine some pages twice . . .
        humming hollowness. Yet one wouldn't willingly have missed
        whole chapters, episodes, pages and paragraphs of this
        extravaganza"

113   wordsworth, christopher *the* (manchester) *guardian* 9/14/62.
        "no doubt about the behemoth talent; the doubts lie in the
        use to which it has been put. . . . Not a sperm-whale, not
        seminal. But incontestably a whale"

---

*sentence is a distortion of 2 passages on p1 above   it annoyed the british
critics but wasnt strong enough to terrify them

114   ricks, christopher *new statesman* (london weekly review)
9/14/62 [330]   "much pretentious sludge.... But even
the bad things have a mad aplomb"

115   *the* (london) *times literary supplement* [by Anthony Cronin]
9/14/62 [685]   "passages of sustained brilliance and
interest which are sometimes more than half the length of
an ordinary novel ... much of the time completely at sea
about what he was doing, and attempting to cover up by
sheer pretentiousness and hokum ... a puzzle, at times a
rewarding one"

116   daniel, john *the spectator* (london weekly review) 9/21/62
[410]   "956 pages is a lot with no development.... The
threads are dazzling, but we step back and there is no
pattern"

JACK GREEN attended Princeton and worked for an insurance company before supporting himself full-time as a freelance proof-reader. Seventeen issues of his *newspaper* appeared between 1957 and 1965.

STEVEN MOORE is an American author and literary critic. Best known as an authority on the novels of William Gaddis, he published the first volume of his major work *The Novel: An Alternative History* in 2010.

Petros Abatzoglou, *What Does Mrs. Freeman Want?*
Michal Ajvaz, *The Golden Age.*
  The Other City.
Pierre Albert-Birot, *Grabinoulor.*
Yuz Aleshkovsky, *Kangaroo.*
Felipe Alfau, *Chromos.*
  Locos.
João Almino, *The Book of Emotions.*
Ivan Ângelo, *The Celebration.*
  The Tower of Glass.
David Antin, *Talking.*
António Lobo Antunes, *Knowledge of Hell.*
  The Splendor of Portugal.
Alain Arias-Misson, *Theatre of Incest.*
Iftikhar Arif and Waqas Khwaja, eds., *Modern Poetry of Pakistan.*
John Ashbery and James Schuyler, *A Nest of Ninnies.*
Robert Ashley, *Perfect Lives.*
Gabriela Avigur-Rotem, *Heatwave and Crazy Birds.*
Heimrad Bäcker, *transcript.*
Djuna Barnes, *Ladies Almanack.*
  Ryder.
John Barth, *LETTERS.*
  Sabbatical.
Donald Barthelme, *The King.*
  Paradise.
Svetislav Basara, *Chinese Letter.*
René Belletto, *Dying.*
Mark Binelli, *Sacco and Vanzetti Must Die!*
Andrei Bitov, *Pushkin House.*
Andrej Blatnik, *You Do Understand.*
Louis Paul Boon, *Chapel Road.*
  My Little War.
  Summer in Termuren.
Roger Boylan, *Killoyle.*
Ignácio de Loyola Brandão, *Anonymous Celebrity.*
  The Good-Bye Angel.
  Teeth under the Sun.
  Zero.
Bonnie Bremser, *Troia: Mexican Memoirs.*
Christine Brooke-Rose, *Amalgamemnon.*
Brigid Brophy, *In Transit.*
Meredith Brosnan, *Mr. Dynamite.*
Gerald L. Bruns, *Modern Poetry and the Idea of Language.*
Evgeny Bunimovich and J. Kates, eds., *Contemporary Russian Poetry: An Anthology.*
Gabrielle Burton, *Heartbreak Hotel.*
Michel Butor, *Degrees.*
  Mobile.
  Portrait of the Artist as a Young Ape.
G. Cabrera Infante, *Infante's Inferno.*
  Three Trapped Tigers.
Julieta Campos, *The Fear of Losing Eurydice.*
Anne Carson, *Eros the Bittersweet.*
Orly Castel-Bloom, *Dolly City.*
Camilo José Cela, *Christ versus Arizona.*
  The Family of Pascual Duarte.
  The Hive.
Louis-Ferdinand Céline, *Castle to Castle.*
  Conversations with Professor Y.
  London Bridge.

Normance.
North.
Rigadoon.
Hugo Charteris, *The Tide Is Right.*
Jerome Charyn, *The Tar Baby.*
Eric Chevillard, *Demolishing Nisard.*
Marc Cholodenko, *Mordechai Schamz.*
Joshua Cohen, *Witz.*
Emily Holmes Coleman, *The Shutter of Snow.*
Robert Coover, *A Night at the Movies.*
Stanley Crawford, *Log of the S.S. The Mrs Unguentine.*
  Some Instructions to My Wife.
Robert Creeley, *Collected Prose.*
René Crevel, *Putting My Foot in It.*
Ralph Cusack, *Cadenza.*
Susan Daitch, *L.C.*
  Storytown.
Nicholas Delbanco, *The Count of Concord.*
  Sherbrookes.
Nigel Dennis, *Cards of Identity.*
Peter Dimock, *A Short Rhetoric for Leaving the Family.*
Ariel Dorfman, *Konfidenz.*
Coleman Dowell, *The Houses of Children.*
  Island People.
  Too Much Flesh and Jabez.
Arkadii Dragomoshchenko, *Dust.*
Rikki Ducornet, *The Complete Butcher's Tales.*
  The Fountains of Neptune.
  The Jade Cabinet.
  The One Marvelous Thing.
  Phosphor in Dreamland.
  The Stain.
  The Word "Desire."
William Eastlake, *The Bamboo Bed.*
  Castle Keep.
  Lyric of the Circle Heart.
Jean Echenoz, *Chopin's Move.*
Stanley Elkin, *A Bad Man.*
  Boswell: A Modern Comedy.
  Criers and Kibitzers, Kibitzers and Criers.
  The Dick Gibson Show.
  The Franchiser.
  George Mills.
  The Living End.
  The MacGuffin.
  The Magic Kingdom.
  Mrs. Ted Bliss.
  The Rabbi of Lud.
  Van Gogh's Room at Arles.
François Emmanuel, *Invitation to a Voyage.*
Annie Ernaux, *Cleaned Out.*
Lauren Fairbanks, *Muzzle Thyself.*
  Sister Carrie.
Leslie A. Fiedler, *Love and Death in the American Novel.*
Juan Filloy, *Op Oloop.*
Gustave Flaubert, *Bouvard and Pécuchet.*
Kass Fleisher, *Talking out of School.*
Ford Madox Ford, *The March of Literature.*
Jon Fosse, *Aliss at the Fire.*
  Melancholy.
Max Frisch, *I'm Not Stiller.*

SELECTED DALKEY ARCHIVE PAPERBACKS

Man in the Holocene.
CARLOS FUENTES, *Christopher Unborn.*
Distant Relations.
Terra Nostra.
Where the Air Is Clear.
WILLIAM GADDIS, *J R.*
The Recognitions.
JANICE GALLOWAY, *Foreign Parts.*
The Trick Is to Keep Breathing.
WILLIAM H. GASS, *Cartesian Sonata*
and Other Novellas.
Finding a Form.
A Temple of Texts.
The Tunnel.
Willie Masters' Lonesome Wife.
GÉRARD GAVARRY, *Hoppla! 1 2 3.*
Making a Novel.
ETIENNE GILSON,
The Arts of the Beautiful.
Forms and Substances in the Arts.
C. S. GISCOMBE, *Giscome Road.*
Here.
Prairie Style.
DOUGLAS GLOVER, *Bad News of the Heart.*
The Enamoured Knight.
WITOLD GOMBROWICZ,
A Kind of Testament.
KAREN ELIZABETH GORDON,
The Red Shoes.
GEORGI GOSPODINOV, *Natural Novel.*
JUAN GOYTISOLO, *Count Julian.*
Exiled from Almost Everywhere.
Juan the Landless.
Makbara.
Marks of Identity.
PATRICK GRAINVILLE, *The Cave of Heaven.*
HENRY GREEN, *Back.*
Blindness.
Concluding.
Doting.
Nothing.
JACK GREEN, *Fire the Bastards!*
JIŘÍ GRUŠA, *The Questionnaire.*
GABRIEL GUDDING,
Rhode Island Notebook.
MELA HARTWIG, *Am I a Redundant*
Human Being?
JOHN HAWKES, *The Passion Artist.*
Whistlejacket.
ALEKSANDAR HEMON, ED.,
Best European Fiction.
AIDAN HIGGINS, *A Bestiary.*
Balcony of Europe.
Bornholm Night-Ferry.
Darkling Plain: Texts for the Air.
Flotsam and Jetsam.
Langrishe, Go Down.
Scenes from a Receding Past.
Windy Arbours.
KEIZO HINO, *Isle of Dreams.*
KAZUSHI HOSAKA, *Plainsong.*
ALDOUS HUXLEY, *Antic Hay.*
Crome Yellow.
Point Counter Point.
Those Barren Leaves.
Time Must Have a Stop.
NAOYUKI II, *The Shadow of a Blue Cat.*
MIKHAIL IOSSEL AND JEFF PARKER, EDS.,
Amerika: Russian Writers View the
United States.
DRAGO JANČAR, *The Galley Slave.*
GERT JONKE, *The Distant Sound.*

Geometric Regional Novel.
Homage to Czerny.
The System of Vienna.
JACQUES JOUET, *Mountain R.*
Savage.
Upstaged.
CHARLES JULIET, *Conversations with*
Samuel Beckett and Bram van
Velde.
MIEKO KANAI, *The Word Book.*
YORAM KANIUK, *Life on Sandpaper.*
HUGH KENNER, *The Counterfeiters.*
Flaubert, Joyce and Beckett:
The Stoic Comedians.
Joyce's Voices.
DANILO KIŠ, *Garden, Ashes.*
A Tomb for Boris Davidovich.
ANITA KONKKA, *A Fool's Paradise.*
GEORGE KONRÁD, *The City Builder.*
TADEUSZ KONWICKI, *A Minor Apocalypse.*
The Polish Complex.
MENIS KOUMANDAREAS, *Koula.*
ELAINE KRAF, *The Princess of 72nd Street.*
JIM KRUSOE, *Iceland.*
EWA KURYLUK, *Century 21.*
EMILIO LASCANO TEGUI, *On Elegance*
While Sleeping.
ERIC LAURRENT, *Do Not Touch.*
HERVÉ LE TELLIER, *The Sextine Chapel.*
A Thousand Pearls (for a Thousand
Pennies)
VIOLETTE LEDUC, *La Bâtarde.*
EDOUARD LEVÉ, *Autoportrait.*
Suicide.
SUZANNE JILL LEVINE, *The Subversive*
Scribe: Translating Latin
American Fiction.
DEBORAH LEVY, *Billy and Girl.*
Pillow Talk in Europe and Other
Places.
JOSÉ LEZAMA LIMA, *Paradiso.*
ROSA LIKSOM, *Dark Paradise.*
OSMAN LINS, *Avalovara.*
The Queen of the Prisons of Greece.
ALF MAC LOCHLAINN,
The Corpus in the Library.
Out of Focus.
RON LOEWINSOHN, *Magnetic Field(s).*
MINA LOY, *Stories and Essays of Mina Loy.*
BRIAN LYNCH, *The Winner of Sorrow.*
D. KEITH MANO, *Take Five.*
MICHELINE AHARONIAN MARCOM,
The Mirror in the Well.
BEN MARCUS,
The Age of Wire and String.
WALLACE MARKFIELD,
Teitlebaum's Window.
To an Early Grave.
DAVID MARKSON, *Reader's Block.*
Springer's Progress.
Wittgenstein's Mistress.
CAROLE MASO, *AVA.*
LADISLAV MATEJKA AND KRYSTYNA
POMORSKA, EDS.,
Readings in Russian Poetics:
Formalist and Structuralist Views.
HARRY MATHEWS,
The Case of the Persevering Maltese:
Collected Essays.
Cigarettes.
The Conversions.
The Human Country: New and

SELECTED DALKEY ARCHIVE PAPERBACKS

Collected Stories.
The Journalist.
My Life in CIA.
Singular Pleasures.
The Sinking of the Odradek
    Stadium.
Tlooth.
20 Lines a Day.
JOSEPH MCELROY,
    Night Soul and Other Stories.
THOMAS MCGONIGLE,
    Going to Patchogue.
ROBERT L. MCLAUGHLIN, ED., Innovations:
    An Anthology of
    Modern & Contemporary Fiction.
ABDELWAHAB MEDDEB, Talismano.
GERHARD MEIER, Isle of the Dead.
HERMAN MELVILLE, The Confidence-Man.
AMANDA MICHALOPOULOU, I'd Like.
STEVEN MILLHAUSER,
    The Barnum Museum.
    In the Penny Arcade.
RALPH J. MILLS, JR.,
    Essays on Poetry.
MOMUS, The Book of Jokes.
CHRISTINE MONTALBETTI, Western.
OLIVE MOORE, Spleen.
NICHOLAS MOSLEY, Accident.
    Assassins.
    Catastrophe Practice.
    Children of Darkness and Light.
    Experience and Religion.
    God's Hazard.
    The Hesperides Tree.
    Hopeful Monsters.
    Imago Bird.
    Impossible Object.
    Inventing God.
    Judith.
    Look at the Dark.
    Natalie Natalia.
    Paradoxes of Peace.
    Serpent.
    Time at War.
    The Uses of Slime Mould:
        Essays of Four Decades.
WARREN MOTTE,
    Fables of the Novel: French Fiction
        since 1990.
    Fiction Now: The French Novel in
        the 21st Century.
    Oulipo: A Primer of Potential
        Literature.
GERALD MURNANE, Barley Patch.
YVES NAVARRE, Our Share of Time.
    Sweet Tooth.
DOROTHY NELSON, In Night's City.
    Tar and Feathers.
ESHKOL NEVO, Homesick.
WILFRIDO D. NOLLEDO, But for the Lovers.
FLANN O'BRIEN,
    At Swim-Two-Birds.
    At War.
    The Best of Myles.
    The Dalkey Archive.
    Further Cuttings.
    The Hard Life.
    The Poor Mouth.
    The Third Policeman.
CLAUDE OLLIER, The Mise-en-Scène.
    Wert and the Life Without End.
PATRIK OUŘEDNÍK, Europeana.

The Opportune Moment, 1855.
BORIS PAHOR, Necropolis.
FERNANDO DEL PASO,
    News from the Empire.
    Palinuro of Mexico.
ROBERT PINGET, The Inquisitory.
    Mahu or The Material.
    Trio.
A. G. PORTA, The No World Concerto.
MANUEL PUIG,
    Betrayed by Rita Hayworth.
    The Buenos Aires Affair.
    Heartbreak Tango.
RAYMOND QUENEAU, The Last Days.
    Odile.
    Pierrot Mon Ami.
    Saint Glinglin.
ANN QUIN, Berg.
    Passages.
    Three.
    Tripticks.
ISHMAEL REED,
    The Free-Lance Pallbearers.
    The Last Days of Louisiana Red.
    Ishmael Reed: The Plays.
    Juice!
    Reckless Eyeballing.
    The Terrible Threes.
    The Terrible Twos.
    Yellow Back Radio Broke-Down.
JOÃO UBALDO RIBEIRO, House of the
    Fortunate Buddhas.
JEAN RICARDOU, Place Names.
RAINER MARIA RILKE, The Notebooks of
    Malte Laurids Brigge.
JULIÁN RÍOS, The House of Ulysses.
    Larva: A Midsummer Night's Babel.
    Poundemonium.
    Procession of Shadows.
AUGUSTO ROA BASTOS, I the Supreme.
DANIËL ROBBERECHTS,
    Arriving in Avignon.
JEAN ROLIN, The Explosion of the
    Radiator Hose.
OLIVIER ROLIN, Hotel Crystal.
ALIX CLEO ROUBAUD, Alix's Journal.
JACQUES ROUBAUD, The Form of a
    City Changes Faster, Alas, Than
    the Human Heart.
    The Great Fire of London.
    Hortense in Exile.
    Hortense Is Abducted.
    The Loop.
    Mathématique:
    The Plurality of Worlds of Lewis.
    The Princess Hoppy.
    Some Thing Black.
LEON S. ROUDIEZ, French Fiction Revisited.
RAYMOND ROUSSEL, Impressions of Africa.
VEDRANA RUDAN, Night.
STIG SÆTERBAKKEN, Siamese.
LYDIE SALVAYRE, The Company of Ghosts.
    Everyday Life.
    The Lecture.
    Portrait of the Writer as a
        Domesticated Animal.
    The Power of Flies.
LUIS RAFAEL SÁNCHEZ,
    Macho Camacho's Beat.
SEVERO SARDUY, Cobra & Maitreya.
NATHALIE SARRAUTE,
    Do You Hear Them?

FOR A FULL LIST OF PUBLICATIONS, VISIT:
www.dalkeyarchive.com

Martereau.
The Planetarium.
Arno Schmidt, *Collected Novellas.*
Collected Stories.
Nobodaddy's Children.
Two Novels.
Asaf Schurr, *Motti.*
Christine Schutt, *Nightwork.*
Gail Scott, *My Paris.*
Damion Searls, *What We Were Doing
and Where We Were Going.*
June Akers Seese,
Is This What Other Women Feel Too?
What Waiting Really Means.
Bernard Share, *Inish.*
Transit.
Aurelie Sheehan,
Jack Kerouac Is Pregnant.
Viktor Shklovsky, *Bowstring.*
Knight's Move.
*A Sentimental Journey:
Memoirs 1917–1922.*
Energy of Delusion: A Book on Plot.
Literature and Cinematography.
Theory of Prose.
Third Factory.
Zoo, or Letters Not about Love.
Claude Simon, *The Invitation.*
Pierre Siniac, *The Collaborators.*
Kjersti A. Skomsvold, *The Faster I Walk,
the Smaller I Am.*
Josef Škvorecký, *The Engineer of
Human Souls.*
Gilbert Sorrentino,
Aberration of Starlight.
Blue Pastoral.
Crystal Vision.
*Imaginative Qualities of Actual
Things.*
Mulligan Stew.
Pack of Lies.
Red the Fiend.
The Sky Changes.
Something Said.
Splendide-Hôtel.
Steelwork.
Under the Shadow.
W. M. Spackman,
The Complete Fiction.
Andrzej Stasiuk, *Dukla.*
Fado.
Gertrude Stein,
Lucy Church Amiably.
The Making of Americans.
A Novel of Thank You.
Lars Svendsen, *A Philosophy of Evil.*
Piotr Szewc, *Annihilation.*
Gonçalo M. Tavares, *Jerusalem.*
Joseph Walser's Machine.
*Learning to Pray in the Age of
Technique.*
Lucian Dan Teodorovici,
Our Circus Presents . . .
Nikanor Teratologen, *Assisted Living.*
Stefan Themerson, *Hobson's Island.*
The Mystery of the Sardine.
Tom Harris.
John Toomey, *Sleepwalker.*
Jean-Philippe Toussaint,
The Bathroom.
Camera.
Monsieur.

Running Away.
Self-Portrait Abroad.
Television.
The Truth about Marie.
Dumitru Tsepeneag,
Hotel Europa.
The Necessary Marriage.
Pigeon Post.
Vain Art of the Fugue.
Esther Tusquets, *Stranded.*
Dubravka Ugresic,
Lend Me Your Character.
Thank You for Not Reading.
Mati Unt, *Brecht at Night.*
Diary of a Blood Donor.
Things in the Night.
Álvaro Uribe and Olivia Sears, eds.,
*Best of Contemporary Mexican
Fiction.*
Eloy Urroz, *Friction.*
The Obstacles.
Luisa Valenzuela, *Dark Desires and
the Others.*
He Who Searches.
Marja-Liisa Vartio,
The Parson's Widow.
Paul Verhaeghen, *Omega Minor.*
Aglaja Veteranyi, *Why the Child Is
Cooking in the Polenta.*
Boris Vian, *Heartsnatcher.*
Llorenç Villalonga, *The Dolls' Room.*
Ornela Vorpsi, *The Country Where No
One Ever Dies.*
Austryn Wainhouse, *Hedyphagetica.*
Paul West,
Words for a Deaf Daughter & Gala.
Curtis White,
America's Magic Mountain.
The Idea of Home.
Memories of My Father Watching TV.
*Monstrous Possibility: An Invitation
to Literary Politics.*
Requiem.
Diane Williams, *Excitability:
Selected Stories.*
Romancer Erector.
Douglas Woolf, *Wall to Wall.*
Ya! & John-Juan.
Jay Wright, *Polynomials and Pollen.*
*The Presentable Art of Reading
Absence.*
Philip Wylie, *Generation of Vipers.*
Marguerite Young, *Angel in the Forest.*
Miss MacIntosh, My Darling.
REYoung, *Unbabbling.*
Vlado Žabot, *The Succubus.*
Zoran Živković, *Hidden Camera.*
Louis Zukofsky, *Collected Fiction.*
Vitomil Zupan, *Minuet for Guitar.*
Scott Zwiren, *God Head.*